Journal It!

Journal It!

Take Hold of Your Life by Journaling

Gwendolyn Carole Tipton

RESOURCE *Publications* • Eugene, Oregon

JOURNAL IT!
Take Hold of Your Life by Journaling

Resource Publications
An Imprint of Wipf and Stock Publishers
199 W. 8th Ave., Suite 3
Eugene, OR 97401

www.wipfandstock.com

PAPERBACK ISBN: 978-1-5326-5840-2
HARDCOVER ISBN: 978-1-5326-5841-9
EBOOK ISBN: 978-1-5326-5842-6

Manufactured in the U.S.A.

For my beloved husband, Robert, and our young adults,
Ryan and Lauren. We are together again.

Contents

Introduction

FOR SOMETHING TO CHANGE in life, one of two things must happen: either life changes or you must make a change. It's up to you. At some point, your life mandates that you "take hold of your life" and transform it " . . . to be made new in the attitude of your minds; and to put on the new self, created to be like God in true righteousness and holiness" (Eph 4:23–24).

This book is meant to support you as you engage in changes. Through journaling, you can step back for a moment, evaluate your life, and determine what you want your ideal life to become. Then, journal your way to the destination, keeping in mind that you must: "Do your best to present yourself to God as one approved, a worker who has no need to be ashamed, rightly handling the word of truth" (2 Tim 2:15).

To start, write your life story from beginning to end with extravagant descriptions and massive details just as you want it. This is the first step in taking hold of your life by journaling. You cannot change the past, but you have the tools to plant and create the future. Writing about you is your chance to review and revise your life, then make changes based on your guidance from God. Listen for his messages and look for his signals for new ventures that offer undertakings beyond your dreams.

You are going to write your story as you want to live it. Write out the pluses and minuses of the limitless life changes you want to make. Create plans to overcome the difficulties and expand upon the opportunities that will help you get to the final chapter. Outline your life story. Begin to write with a spirit of hope. "For whatever was written in former days was written for our instruction, that through endurance and through the encouragement of the Scriptures we might have hope" (Rom 15:4).

This is what happened today . . . It's all about you in your space at your place. Your opinions are the only ones that matter. Choose a place to write what is worth describing carefully in your journal. Every day there is a happening that must be included in your journal. The more exciting the event, the more space it takes in your journal.

Taking hold of your life and having hold of your life are very crucial principles.

As an adult, you are solely responsible for your choices. Many people blame others or circumstances for the things that are not right in their lives. When we analyze the past, we recognize exactly what brought on the situation and how it was or was not resolved. We often forget that it is from our mistakes that we learn the most. If we deny our mistakes or fail to take responsibility, we fail to improve. "If we confess our sins, he is faithful and just to forgive us our sins and to cleanse us from all unrighteousness" (1 John 1:9).

Most people make mistakes and try again. Every mistake and every catastrophe are life-changing experiences. They are part of your life story in which the forgiveness of God represents a blessing.

We must journal our stories day by day. Reread, review, and then we can rewrite the story by getting hold of our lives, by getting out there, by not being terrified of making mistakes, by learning from past chapters of our lives as we embrace each moment as an opportunity to learn and do better. "Commit to the Lord whatever you do, and he will establish your plans. The Lord works out everything to its proper end" (Prov 16:3–4).

We must also recognize we are responsible for the way we respond to people, actions, and events in our lives. In fact, in my view, one of the key determinants of how we perform in life is not defined by what actually happens to us, but rather how we respond to the events God puts in our way. Chronicling those daily experiences will allow us to assess our progress, or lack thereof, toward the goal.

As you get your honest thoughts down on paper, you can clarify what you like about yourself and what you want to change. You are responsible for your today! Tomorrow is in the hands of God. "Do not be anxious about anything, but in every situation, by prayer and petition, with thanksgiving, present your requests to God" (Phil 4:6).

Journal it and take hold to change your life going forward. You only need a writing instrument and paper on which to write a journal, and the commitment to yourself that you will journal. If you are dedicated, you will experiment until you establish a pace and place that feels good and demands that you write something, at an appointed time.

And pray. Dear Lord, take and receive my whole life, all that I am and all I want to be. You made me. Now take me back and use me according to your will. Give me the tenacity and discipline to follow through so that ultimately, you will "create in me a pure heart, O God, and renew a steadfast spirit within me" (Ps 51:10).

The Scriptures used in this book are taken from the Holy Bible, New International Version (NIV).

Chapter 1—What is Journaling?

"Then the Lord replied: Write down the revelation
and make it plain on tablets so that a herald may run with it.
For the revelation awaits an appointed time;
it speaks of the end and will not prove false.
Though it linger, wait for it; it will certainly come and will not delay."

HABAKKUK 2:2–3

Prayer: Heavenly Father, I am writing to encourage others to write reflections from you to help them transform their lives. Guide me as I write words that may reveal your messages for others. Thank you for the opportunity to share your word. Amen.

"JOURNAL" COMES FROM THE French word *jour*, meaning "day," as in soup *du jour* or soup of the day. A journal represents a record of your opinions, occurrences, and annotations during one day. You can write in your journal when you feel the need to clarify an issue or simply record happenings.

Journaling to change your life requires more than periodic writing. Many people will put it off or not start or wait for inspiration that may not come until they have developed a purpose for journaling or a specific need for a long-lost stimulation.

Today, since journaling is so popular, it is a term used for the practice of keeping a diary that explores thoughts and feelings surrounding the events of one's life. Journaling can be a stress-management tool, a self-correction tool, or a self-exploration tool, which is more than simply recording the happenings of the day or keeping a log. To help get hold of your life, you must write in detail about all the feelings related to occurrences or people, much as one would discuss topics with a therapist.

Journaling is more personal than a diary. It contains feelings, emotions, problems, self-assurances, and plans for the future. We are using it to change your life based on how it reads to you. In addition to the descriptive writing, we want to include thoughts, attitudes, and reflections.

Definitions

Diary: a record of events, transactions, or observations kept daily or at frequent intervals, journal; a daily record of personal activities, reflections, or feelings, a book intended or used for a diary.

Journal: a record of current transactions; especially: a book of original entry in double-entry bookkeeping; an account of day-to-day events; a record of experiences, ideas, or reflections kept regularly for private use.

A journal and a diary are used interchangeably, but for this discussion, we are saying a diary is more of a log of events—where did you go, what did you do, and so on. A journal, on the other hand, is a more personal reflection on who you are, what you feel, and how you can improve your life.

Both are referred to as books. You can buy a blank diary or a journal and they may both look the same. Make sure it's not gold lamé or something too fancy, which may be too pretty to mess up with writing.

You don't have to purchase anything to get started. You need a writing instrument that feels good in your hand. I like a fine-point ink pen. You need a small notepad, spiral notebook, three-ring notebook, bound journal, lined paper, grid paper, paper, whatever feels right. Or, you may prefer electronic journaling on your personal computer, smartphone, tablet, or app. I use special folders on my Mac mini computer.

With tools in hand, it's time to create the habit of journaling. My advice is simple: have a set time, be it before breakfast, after dinner, before you go to bed, whenever. But, it must be a task that has no excuses. Promise yourself to journal.

I journal, but I also include my prayers to ensure that I account for my feelings and actions as in a diary when writing. This way I paint a picture of not only who I am but also who I want to become. So, whether you keep a journal, diary, or a hybrid like I do, most of the tips and suggestions in this book are equally applicable. Fill your journal with words of meaning to you.

Just remember "that everyone will have to give account on the day of judgment for every empty word they have spoken" (Matt 12:36).

Six Facets of Journaling

i. Planning: Make a plan to journal your implementation process, including successes and failures. Or, plan a trip with pre-travel activities, photos during the travel, destination pleasures, and memorable events. I use several journals, all of which have a directive that includes the date and specific prompt words so I can stay on point. Since I try to maintain an attitude of gratitude, my first prompt is "Thanks for this day that went well. I accomplished _____."

ii. Focusing: Concentrate on a specific project, such as home decorating, landscaping, building a new wardrobe, healthy eating, books to read, or relationship management. My reading project is to read three books per month: one classic, one bestseller, and one how-to. In my book journal, I post the date, book title, genre, a brief paragraph about the book, and give it my personal rating.

iii. Testing Yourself: Journal your achievements, or absence of them, for example: losing weight, exercising habits, spending management, and savings growth. Writing about these test results in my diary wasn't getting the job done. Thus, I made a separate chart to post my daily activities to monitor them.

iv. Monitoring activities and actions: List the time and make notes when something significant happens. Since I spend too much money on small purchases, I have a two-by-three-inch notebook, where I write down every cent I spend and on what. I look at it daily as it seems like the money is falling out of my pockets.

v. Memorializing: Store tickets of events, dinner menus, newspaper articles, drawings, cards, and programs, as well as photos taken. I enjoy saving cards that I received for Christmas, my birthday, as thank-yous, and for other occasions. I keep them by year and each one has a written memory related to that card-deserving event.

vi. Expressing your gratitude: Say thank you in a gratitude journal by acknowledging miracles, wonders, and blessings. My gratitude journal is part of my master journal, which is spiritual and filled with prayers requests and thanksgiving.

There are myriad areas on which to focus a journal, whether it be something that is in your heart or your mind, or a dream you want to make come true.

You can and should make rules for journaling. Here are my rules to help me write about all the things that create my personal life's tapestry. When I'm honest about my feelings, it is like mental conditioning. It's not necessary to use all of the rules during every session, but rules are like guidelines to ensure I'm on the correct path to getting hold of my life by journaling. "But test them all; hold on to what is good" (1 Thess 5:21).

1. Write to express your personal values as you see them.

2. Write about your best life and your worst life.

3. Write from your heart, as if you expect to be heard by the giver of your needs.

4. Write with confidence as you reveal private thoughts only for you.

5. Write about your passion and purpose in life.

6. Write about pain inflicted by others and by you.

7. Write about your stresses.

8. Write your prayer requests and your blessings.

9. Write for a specific time each designated day—ten to sixty minutes, for example—without stopping.

10. Write on a schedule for several weeks before taking a break to establish a routine.

We accept that a journal represents a record of your opinions, occurrences, and annotations during one day. Therefore, we should keep a journal because God keeps a record, according to Psalm 56:8: "Record my misery; list my tears on your scroll—are they not in your record?"

Assignment:

- Select a writing instrument that writes well for you.

- Select a journal that reflects your taste.

- Select a time and place to write.

- Make a list of three or more areas on which you would like to focus your journal.

- Make your list of three or more rules for journaling.

Chapter 2—Benefits of Journaling

"Keep my commands and you will live;
guard my teachings as the apple of your eye. Bind them
on your fingers; write them on the tablet of your heart."

PROVERBS 7:2–3

Prayer: Heavenly Father, I try very hard to keep your commandments and exemplify your word. Renew your spirit in my heart that I may share your word though journaling to spread your teachings. Thank you for letting me live in your favor. Amen.

JOURNALING ALLOWS YOU TO clarify your thoughts and feelings, thereby gaining valuable self-knowledge. It can ease stress and improve your mood, especially if the writing is about something enjoyable and positive. It's also a good problem-solving tool; oftentimes, you can hash out a problem and come up with solutions more easily on paper. Putting your dreams in print makes them sacred. The extravagance of your dreams is in your mind. The more you write about them, the closer they are to reality.

Journaling about traumatic events helps us process them by fully examining the feelings related to the occurrence. Writing them down helps control the emotions that are attached to the negative experience, as it takes time to think about the situation and then write about it with the feelings at hand.

When dealing with an unexpected medical diagnosis or illness or death, writing about it can help you journey through the storm. Every day, more and more pain is described, and then once it is out it's time to move on to less painful thoughts and then to mediocre thoughts that pass the time away. Once the negative writings have been exhausted, the pleasant aspects of life will come forth again, whether they are past memories or future goals.

Because you are writing about what is important to you and how you feel about it, you address problems and say what's on your mind and describe what's in your heart. Major events may take days and pages. Yet small events can take up the same amount of space. Regardless of the words or lack of them, write for an hour or two or three or until you've reached a satisfactory conclusion or plan for the next day or encounter.

Writing about something positive or wonderful will enhance your writing skills as you will naturally be very specific with your descriptions. It's like laughter: it just comes out filled with emotion and physical responses like tears, touching a nearby person, smiling at a stranger, slapping your leg or arm, or getting out of your chair to walk around and calm yourself. Describing such joyful movements takes a lot of words and time. Job 8:21 says, "He will yet fill your mouth with laughter and your lips with shouts of joy."

Some occasions require time and feelings, for example, the birth of your first child, another infant added to the family, marriage, holiday family gatherings and social affairs. You want to remember them as they occurred. You probably have photographs to go with your writings. Or then again, you may want to compose new words to plainly portray the happenings through your eyes and how you are presently feeling about them.

Jotting down brilliant ideas that come into your head can be the beginning of an inspiration or a dream. If it is in writing, you can review and revise it over and over. Dreams can be accomplished when attacked one step at a time. As those steps come into view, it is important to put them in your journal. This demands that you have your journal at hand at all times so the dreams can thrive and ultimately become alive.

Complicated problems require writing down, at a minimum, the pluses and minuses. Noting the pluses and minuses may help clear up confusion in order to develop a clear path toward the ultimate goal. Listing questions that need answering may lead to new and different strategies. As you read it out loud, you can add thoughts that are coming too quickly. A small recorder may be necessary to capture those rapidly firing ideas that are taking you to the next level of the issue. A chart may help you make adjustments and envision progress or failure whether it is personal or business.

Implementing plans requires a separate writing space to monitor what is taking place. Those victories must be applauded and celebrated in print. The mishaps need to be examined at the same time you are going through the plan. Your journal helps you accomplish your goals by standing as a watchdog over your shoulder. Ultimately, success and happiness are part of your goals. Since all of the steps are in the plan, the journal is where you visualize and affirm wishes.

Writing down the foods you eat during the day is a proven method to promote weight loss and to help keep the weight off. It is a simple procedure that can help you understand your eating habits and target problem areas you may have. It is important to be honest with yourself when recording food items and amounts. The food journal can act like a mirror by revealing in print what goes into your body. It can be a very useful tool if done for a period of time. For example, in addition to date, time, and place, some specific titles may include food items, condiments, hunger feelings, beverages, and activities while eating.

If it is a healing journal, it may include clear descriptions of the trauma and what it takes to make it through a day. Writing about whatever and then acting it out can give you the power to change your life.

No matter what your reasons are for journaling and your expected benefits, remember: "my God will meet all your needs according to the riches of his glory in Christ Jesus" (Phil 4:19).

Journaling Counteracts Many Negative Effects of Stress

It is said that the death of a spouse is one of life's most stressful events, followed by divorce and marital separation. This clearly supports the concept that relationships with those we love are the most important parts of our lives. Given that it takes a huge amount of time to get through those events, it takes even more time to write about them. Yet even as the event subsides, the stress may still be present. Now it is time to take a closer look at all the aspects of what happened. Journaling can help write your book of feelings about the event and help quell the painful sensations and move you to your next phase of life.

Writing about difficult stressful occurrences brings you down. It may not feel good to write about your spouse's death on the day after the funeral. You may need to just breathe for a while. Writing about joyful occurrences or dreams is uplifting. Shortly after a spouse's death, a friend announces an upcoming wedding. Now the time has come to expound on today's blissful news and to write about plans for tomorrow's happiness. A heartfelt note to your deceased spouse might be in order.

People who don't fit into the American majority (whether by race, religion, or sexual orientation) can have unique stressors to write about. Describing how you feel allows you to cope with one item at a time and collect a list of tools to use to get through the stressor, with a goal to smile about it when rereading that particular paragraph. Writing can soothe the pain and sharpen the tools you need to use, with a goal to make it disappear.

Writing about the stressors is like acting them out with you playing the part of the good guy and the bad one. This role-playing provides insight that leads to understanding. You can play both roles in your journal. When the pain hits, stop, journal it. You don't need to commit to journaling every day, but just when the stressor hits.

Write until it feels better. You may need to break for a beverage because your throat is getting dry as you expel your feelings onto paper.

Now you have it in print, the happy and the sad. Now what?

Plan a scenario that could help prevent that stressor from appearing again. Consider the people involved in the particular time, space, and place. Organize a strategy to overcome the stressor in a positive way. List all of the positive things that happened before and after the stressor.

Remember your last laugh and belt it out again. It was heartily funny. End this writing session by answering the question: Do I feel better or shall I write more to exhale? You have all the tools to move on. Journal it!

Journaling may or may not release tension from your body like yoga or physical relaxation, but the more you write about a stressor and analyze and evaluate it, the better you will feel. You have the opportunity to adapt to it or delete it, but "Stand firm, and you will win life" (Luke 21:19).

Therapeutic Journaling

Taking hold of your life by journaling can be a life-changing experience by charting a new direction with purpose. You can examine your inner self and then develop a more fulfilling life designed by you. As part of treatment plans, some psychologists use journal-writing therapy to bring about awareness of mental health conditions through using specific prompts to intentionally recognize internal and external conflicts.

Psychologist Dr. Ira Progoff created journal therapy in the 1960s at Drew University in New Jersey, and his intensive journaling method introduced the therapeutic potential of journal writing to the public.

Journaling allows you to capture internal thoughts and feelings without worrying about external judgment from others. You can dialogue and analyze your issues and concerns.

Taking hold of your life may require immediate change and long-term growth to develop a new sense of self. Using written sentences to describe your feelings can stimulate new approaches to problems and new plans for the future.

When you are away from a safe haven, having a pen and paper handy and writing about the surroundings can relieve the anxiety you feel. Writing can become therapeutic when you're having difficulty processing feelings and thoughts. Daydreaming in a journal helps you get through those impossible wait times. When you have your journals with you, they are also good reading to track your progress and check your processes.

Dr. James W. Pennebaker has research that shows writing for fifteen to twenty minutes per day for four consecutive days has a beneficial effect on people, such as immune system changes and terminal illnesses.[1] His concept is that writing about disturbed emotions brings forth healing by allowing pent-up thoughts and feelings to be expressed. Writing mandates that you sit still and concentrate on the page by focusing, understanding, translating, organizing, analyzing, processing, confessing, and connecting. Use your God-given gifts from the Holy Spirit as "there are different kinds of gifts. But they are all given to believers by the same Spirit" (1 Cor 12:4–5).

One phenomenal benefit is to spend more time with yourself. Get to know yourself better. After all, you are your own best friend with whom you can tout your gifts, share your deepest secrets, or envision your incredible dreams of success.

Assignment

- Select a pen that you like and some paper or a journal.

- Journal three days in a row without stopping for at least fifteen minutes.

- Note the length of time you wrote and what you wrote about.

- On day four, determine if you felt better after journaling about a stressor or something negative affecting your life.

- On day five, decide if you have more to say about anything.

1. James W. Pennebaker, *The Writing to Heal: A Guided Journal for Recovering from Trauma and Emotional Upheaval* (Oakland, CA: New Harbinger, 2004), 17–25.

Chapter 3—Get Ready to Journal

"May these words of my mouth and this meditation of my heart
be pleasing in your sight, Lord, my Rock and my Redeemer."

PSALM 19:14

Prayer: Heavenly Father, I am preparing to tell all who
will listen about writing words of meditation in a journal. Give me words that speak inspiration to those who
seek to change their lives. Thank you for being my rock.
Amen.

CREATE YOUR HABIT OF journaling. You decide your habit. Set a
time and place that fit you. I write every day, as I am aspiring
to be an award-winning author, therefore there are no exceptions.
I must write every day. If I am moving around or not at my desk,
where I prefer to write, I make notes to help me describe a reccur-
ring event, a new dream, something funny to include in my next
speech. My advice is simple: have a set time, before breakfast, after
dinner, before you go to bed, whenever. But, it must be a task that
cannot be relegated.

Promise yourself to journal it. Whatever your purpose for
journaling, it cannot be accomplished without a commitment to
write. Make it easy on yourself and reset your priorities as you may
need to give up some other activity. No new endeavor can be accomplished without an obligation to fulfill it. Consider this as your

time for you and you alone. When you don't feel like writing at your appointed time, simply stare at the top of the page and write, "I have nothing to say about anything, because _____." More than likely, at your next sitting you will have something to write, because you will have thought about it over and over.

Journal writing can be helpful when you're struck with overwhelming emotional conditions. Consider the following descriptive words as they may give you inspiration for what to write about.

- Anxiety
- Nervousness
- Unhappiness/happiness
- Sorrow
- Prolonged illness
- Mistreatment
- Disarray
- Overweight/underweight
- Love-hate relationship
- Reconciliation
- Problems
- Personal pain

"Set your minds on things above, not on earthly things" (Col 3:2).

Journaling to Recover

There is limited research literature on journaling. However, as mentioned earlier, therapeutic journaling is becoming a useful tool for psychologists and school counselors.

Journaling can help you get over a negative event. A letter to a person whom you cannot get out of your thoughts may help start the day, whether you mail it or not.

There are many creative and effective ways that journaling can help you recover from bad feelings. Proverbs 15:13 says, "A happy heart makes a face cheerful, but heartache crushes the spirit."

Here are some examples:

- Photographs: Look at the photos that you enjoy, and express your feelings by determining why they make you smile, why the people are happy, why the photo was taken, and why they are in that position or touching one another in certain ways.

- Letters: Write a cheerful letter to someone you dislike. Write to someone you don't know but admire. Write a letter to a deceased parent, grandparent, or friend to tell them about the difficulties you're going through.

- Prompt Sentences: Finish open-ended sentences that relate to any issue that is bothering you, such as, "Today, I am worried about . . . " or "I have trouble sleeping when . . . " or "I miss my brother because . . . " or "I know he/she doesn't like me. I think it's because . . . "

- Self-Dialogue: Choose a person you need to talk to about a difficult subject and write a dialogue between both of you. Construct a conversation with full sentences.

Recovery is difficult under all circumstances, but we must remember that when it seems to be failing, "Then you will call on me and come and pray to me, and I will listen to you. You will seek me and find me when you seek me with all your heart" (Jer 29:12–13).

Here are Fifty Ways to Tackle Journaling

There are many ways to tackle journaling that go beyond writing. The point of getting hold of your life by journaling is to do it in a way that gets you to where you want to be. Since it's all about you, use the tools that help you get in touch with yourself in the best way to capture your emotions, dreams, or challenges.

With some of these tools, you must be engaged in a private place of your own where you can laugh, cry, dance, or sing about it. Once the journal has begun, hide it in a secure location that is truly your hiding place, because it is for your eyes only.

A blank paper and pen offer an opportunity to take a stab at writing a few words or a sentence or two, and write for a few minutes about whatever is on your mind or issues that made the day or destroyed it.

1. Write in a conversational tone as though you are telling a secret to a trusted friend. Spit it out. Just say it.

2. Write precise details to explain a situation clearly with great specificity. Review it at a later time and compare the writing to your memory. It may be different.

3. Write stories about problems that you solve as if it is going to be a movie. Include the drama. Write your story so that it can become an interesting movie script.

4. Write persuasively to change your mind about an issue or present both sides of the debate going on in your mind. Convince yourself that your dream is achievable.

5. Write one or two sentences that capture the gist of what happened during the day. Review it tomorrow so it can help you make plans for the next day.

6. Write creative questions that encourage you to do research and find answers to your wonderings. For example, how much will this venture cost? How long will it take?

7. Write summaries of your day in twenty words or less. When journaling gets boring, limiting the number of words moves the task along and very little time is spent.

8. Write one word per day, in giant letters, that says it all. One word may also start a paragraph or two. One word for the meal may be scrumptious. One word for the restaurant may be beautiful. One word for the company may be delightful.

9. Writing new words each day may require research to explain your message. If your goal is to increase your vocabulary

while you think you're losing words in your mind, this is a good tool.

10. Write poems for the day's journey. Poems make songs. It can become your favorite self-expression for a specific emotion or feeling. It can be something that arouses memories of the past or foretells the future.

11. Write complete descriptions of where you want to be next year on this date. Make it a short story that fictionalizes your dream and includes where you are today, with a few good memories of the past.

12. Write a text that screams out your feelings for the day and explains why you are in this or that kind of mood.

13. Weekdays can stimulate memories related to the day of the week. Write something that starts with each letter, such as Sunday.

> For example:
>
> **S**omething happened at church that brought me joy. The choir sang my favorite song.
>
> **U**nless I get home in time to fix lunch, we will have to dine at Parker's for brunch. Good.
>
> **N**o one spoke of the pastor's wife, who was not in church today. Hmmm.
>
> **D**o not forget to call Mrs. Green's daughter as she is in the hospital.
>
> **A**s I was driving to church, my car was making strange noises under the hood. I must call my mechanic ASAP.
>
> **Y**es. It was a good day at church, and I had a restful day reading the paper and starting a new book.

14. Use things that don't require writing. Simply make a few notes and talk to yourself. A famed excuse is that I don't write well or spell well and did not do well in creative writing classes. Forget the past and try something new.

15. Smartphones all have the app store, which has hundreds of daily journals, sketchbook journals, notebooks, diaries, and more to keep you returning to capture your thoughts.

16. Photo journals confirm your thoughts as you capture something significant that has bearing on your emotions, memories, and dreams. Beside each photo, post a description of the memory it brings forth or the feeling it still captures.

17. Framed photographs of people whom you wish to emulate can be hanging in a prominent location where you will see them daily. Post something you did that reminded you of them and your dreams of being like each one of them.

18. Smash Books. Smash Booking is a scrapbook look-a-like. With a notebook, pen, and glue-stick in hand, you can include unplanned and on-the-move writing, and post photos and memorabilia. I pasted the funeral service program of a friend who committed suicide in my Smash Book and wrote him a note about how much I will miss him.

19. Thermometers drawn with clear degree numbers can be used to show your opinion of your emotions for the day, whether you were cold, warm, or hot. Most people are most comfortable at 75 degrees, which is where you can put a star and every day you feel your best, post a star. Post a red mark when you're feeling down.

20. Calendars provide a method for documenting events and plans on the correct days. Whatever the challenge, dates are germane to when something began or when it ended.

21. Newspaper clippings prove what happened at certain times and can serve as a description of the current status of your dream or plan. I'm dying to write a cookbook. All the stars are writing them, even Gwyneth Paltrow and Oprah Winfrey, whose new book was featured in today's newspaper. I clipped the article for safe keeping.

22. Collectibles require more space, so gather a box for them and describe them, noting the date and the place of the

acquisition. You may need a photograph of the contents to ensure you can remember and identify them, as they may be in a box on the top shelf.

23. A USB flash drive is a perfect place to store jokes, stories, and poems in a private creative journal for safe keeping, and to avoid losing your carefully crafted thoughts. Since I keep my journal on my computer, it is imperative that I back it up daily and use a thumb drive as a second source.

24. Speak your journal out loud. Speak into your smartphone or a recorder to create a recorded journal. When listening, you will discover much from the quality of your tone of voice and the terminology you use.

25. Draw cartoons that put a face, expression, and action to a specific occurrence.

26. Clip cartoons to describe a happening in your life that clearly state how you feel about a specific subject.

27. Interview friends and family members and record the interview as part of gathering information for your memoir.

28. Sketch anything that depicts your current feelings, events of the day, or a perfect dream that you want to remember.

29. Look at journaling differently. Consider your surroundings, your environment, and new tools.

30. Change your scenery periodically to help move you into a journaling mood. Go to a special place on the porch, at the coffee shop, in bed, or at your desk.

31. Choose a ritual such as squatting, doing exercises, putting on a special garment, using a special pen or listening to specific music before you begin to write.

32. Mind maps draw graphical pictures to present information that helps you to examine, reminisce, and create new ideas.

33. Colored pencils can represent the meaning of your mood color; yellow, for example, is the color of sunshine and relates to joy, happiness, intellect, and energy.

34. Complete lyrics or lines from your favorite song to describe the day. Or write a new song.

35. Instant messaging chats can be memorialized and filed in your smartphone or printed and filed in a journal.

36. Clipping one-of-a-kind pictures from magazines can capture the sentiments and happenings of a time period to describe in your journal.

37. News quotes from television and radio sum up unforgettable news and events that may impact your life.

38. Journey journals help you record your travels. Use the recorder on your smartphone while driving to speak your thoughts about the environment and surrounding happenings you want to remember.

39. Travel journals certify the reality of a trip with photos, ticket stubs, receipts, and memorabilia.

40. Speaking a dream into a recorder helps to capture it before it takes flight from your mind. Speak about as much of the dream as you can recall and later describe it in writing to see if it made sense as a concept or a story.

41. Adult coloring books are used to move to a place of peace. While coloring on one page, place a piece of paper nearby to make notations regarding thoughts and ideas that you want to remember.

42. Chalk boards or white boards are popular places for messaging and communicating with others in a household. Make notes on the chalkboard to remind you to journal about a specific subject.

43. Daily Bible devotionals can inspire distinctive subjects for a journal to enhance the reason for a personal undertaking, or to give guidance to the new and diverse sides of you.

44. Journal mapping with a map of the United States is perfect when trying to change your environment. Choose new cities

and determine what, when, where, why, and how they could meet your needs if you visit or consider moving.

45. Partnering with a soulmate will provide good company and conversation as you start the day with a pleasant hello and voice your feelings and plans for the day. Your thoughts are journaled in your memories of one another.

46. Coffee, tea, or milk tastes different some days, even when you drink from the same container. When it smells or looks different, it's time to take notice and journal how you're feeling and why. Determine if it's physical or mental.

47. Coaching yourself involves describing why you need a change, confirming the change is a reality, and involving others who can help, may lead to a winning outcome.

48. Money tracking tells you a lot about your life and how you live it. Make a chart and list every cent you spend and for what reason, and examine it periodically to help determine your financial position or what you want it to be.

49. Hang tablets and pens to journal in spots where you sit in your home, for example in the bathroom, bedroom, kitchen, and near the television. When the thought hits, jot it down quickly to avoid wasting the time necessary to go and get a pen and paper to write. Collect these periodically and incorporate them into one of your journals.

50. Handwriting tells you about your personality and feelings. Examine your handwriting in your journal and make notes on what it is saying to you about your feelings and emotions.

Commit to using some methodology to journal at least three times per week.

Surely some journaling technique is interesting enough for you to want to do it at least three times a week, if not every day. Incorporating your journal writing or remembering into something you enjoy will make a commitment to consistency easier to maintain.

Even though I am not a photographer, using my smartphone to take photos of things I want to remember to write about makes me eager to click often, no matter where I am. I like speaking into my smartphone recoder in the car while driving around the city, especially when I have thoughts that must be journaled. At all times, I have a pen and small notebook (two-by-three-inch) in my purse or pocket to jot down my thoughts.

We will continue to discuss determining the purpose of your journaling and suggest prompts and challenges to get you started.

I know of no drawbacks to journaling. Everyone who wants to do it can do so. Computers have made reading and writing tasks so accessible that a second grader, the disabled, and the elderly can journal with confidence. There is online journaling, word processing programs, digital voice recorders, cell phone recorders and Braille journals. There is no need to be concerned with grammar and spelling, it's your life's work. Plus, it's a most inexpensive way to entertain yourself with pen and paper.

Since we must all be accountable for our life at the final judgment, why not start the journal using a methodology that pleases you. "So then, each of us will give an account of himself to God" (Romans 14:12).

Assignment

- Select four days to journal within the next seven days.
- Select four approaches from the fifty above that look interesting.
- Use a different tactic on each of the four days.
- After completing the four different styles, determine which one to use next week.

Chapter 4—Spiritual Journaling

"But when you pray, go into your room, close the door
and pray to your Father, who is unseen. Then your
Father, who sees what is done in secret, will reward you."

MATTHEW 6:6

Prayer: Heavenly Father, I enjoy sitting at my desk writing meditative prayers in my journal. Help me to discipline myself to write daily for a period of time. Thank you for being with me in private when I write and pray. Amen.

S PIRITUAL JOURNALING IS A reflection on the past, an examination of the now, and a look toward the future. It is your conversation with your God.

There are hundreds of verses in the Bible that address writing as a facet of prayer and worship or imply the need to keep prayers in your memory or a journal. Here are a few.

- 1 John 1:4—"These things we write, so that our joy may be complete."

- Isa 30:8—"Now go, write it on a tablet before them, and inscribe it on a scroll that it may serve in the time to come as a witness forever."

- Jer 30:2—"Thus says the Lord, the God of Israel, 'Write all the words which I have spoken to you in a book.'"

- 1 John 5:14—"This is the confidence we have in approaching God: that if we ask anything according to his will, he hears us."

- 1 Chr 16:11—"Look to the Lord and his strength; seek his face always."

- Eph 6:18—"And pray in the Spirit on all occasions with all kinds of prayers and requests. With this in mind, be alert and always keep on praying for all the Lord's people."

- Rev 1:19—"Therefore write the things which you have seen, and the things which are, and the things which will take place after these things."

Based on biblical references, we accept traditional forms of worship that include prayer, singing, music, reading the Bible, writing about the Bible, going to church, and living a godly life. Worship involves speaking, listening, writing, and doing everything with the heart, mind, and body.

In my book, *The Prayor: One Who Prays*, the mandate is to write your own daily prayer in a journal based on a specific Bible verse and prayer. Prompts are provided to help focus on the essential parts of prayer, which are to pray for others and yourself, ask for forgiveness, and thank God for his blessings. Putting your thoughts in writing is the beginning of a conversation with God. It is much more powerful than a simple spoken prayer. You have a record. Writing helps you focus and clarify your praises and your requests. Reviewing daily writings keeps you in frequent contact with God and through these conversations, your relationship with him grows. Here are examples of Bible verses and prayers in response to them, from my book.

Isaiah 25:1

Lord, you are my God;
I will exalt you and praise your name,

for in perfect faithfulness

you have done wonderful things,

things planned long ago.

Prayer: Sovereign Lord, I sing your praise in words and song. Hourly, I become aware of new experiences. Show me how to triumph over suffering and sorrow. Show me how to join in the praise. Thank you for being my judge, my refuge, and my host. Amen.[1]

Revelation 2:28–29

I will also give him the morning star.

He who has an ear, let him hear what

the Spirit says to the Churches.

Prayer: Sovereign One, each day when I pray intensely, I am counting on seeing the next morning. Speak loudly so that I can hear your word. Thank you in advance for steering me to your temple. Amen.[2]

Keeping a spiritual journal is part of praying and worshipping frequently and intentionally. Keeping a gratitude journal is commonplace, some even think it's corny or silly, but I believe focusing on what we're grateful for allows us to regain perspective and a sense of control over the events that move through our lives. Therefore, having an unrelenting faith allows you to write your reactions in situations where you have no control, while standing tall and believing that things are going to be all right. For such faith, I am grateful. Faith is indeed, "the substance of things hoped for and the evidence of things not seen" (Heb 11:1).

As I try to be a good person and keep his commandments, I believe he will wash my sins away. But he has high standards. If I rob a bank, he will forgive me and still bestow his grace and mercy

1. Gwendolyn Carole Tipton, *The Prayor: One Who Prays* (Bloomington, IN: Westbow, 2013), 28.

2. Tipton, *Prayor*, 364.

upon me, but I have to pay for that wrongdoing. Afterward, I must lift up myself and charge out to live another day. I want to have a relationship with God through prayer and worship. Maintaining that relationship is like maintaining clean bodies. We wash daily with soap and other additives so we can be free of dirt and grime. For my uncleanliness, I ask him throughout each day to wash me clean so that I may be without stain or blemish when he comes for me.

In the meantime, in faith, I humbly wait for his grace and mercy, for I cannot live without it. In my journal, I call upon him every day. I "pray continually" (1 Thess 5:17).

Spiritual Journals May Include Pages to . . .

- Tie your writing to your readings about God in spiritual books and the Bible.

  I write: Dear Heavenly Father, sometimes I don't recognize your miracles and signs of your presence. Teach me to always believe in your wonders and share them with my children and grandchildren, who are most important to me. I pray for prosperity and with such, help me to share with others my gifts in love and gratitude as they have brought me joy. Thank you for guiding me to remain your humble servant. Amen.

- Keep you in touch with God by writing daily and reviewing daily while listening, watching, and waiting for his direction.

  I write: Come to me, Lord Jesus, send me your spirit. Create in me a clean heart. In your whisper last night, I heard you tell me to visit several people whom I've known for many years, just to say hello. My response is to call each one and put them on my calendar for a visit. In the meantime, I will buy gifts that will give them something to do, such as an audiobook, stimulating games, and puzzles, movies, or a flowering plant that needs care. Amen.

- Record the miracles, signs, and wonders that you witness.

I write: Thank God for Dee's body that is growing stronger each day with his new heart. From the first day I was asked to pray for him, I had initial doubts as he was in his early forties and not high on the waiting list for a heart in South Carolina. Thank you for the heart, for guiding the physicians and caregivers, for his lovely wife standing by, for his calling and reporting to say he felt fine. Thank God for this miracle. Amen.

- Thank God for his blessings and ways of sharing.

    I write: Praise God for his many blessings and I pray that Cousin Mollie will plan and organize a family gathering in the coming year for the children, grand-children, and elderly cousins. Because they live in many different locations, coming together is expensive. I pray that I can search my bank accounts to collect enough money to help John and Rea, who married last year and are now with a baby and mom at home. Guide me Lord with your provision. Amen.

- Maintain specific prayers of focus on a special need, such as peace of mind.

    I write: Lord Jesus, I am praying for peace in my mind. Let neither the disease of dementia nor Alzheimer's attack me. Heal the things in my life that are causing me stress, like grief and sorrow for the loss of family members and friends. Let my family members who are at odds with one another be at peace with each other and with me. Let your peace reign in our families, at the places where I volunteer, and with everyone I touch with my hands or with your spirit. Amen.

- Count your blessings and see what God has done.

    I write: Heavenly Father, I am blessed as you continue to show such favor on me and the lady prayer warriors with whom I pray every Saturday morning. And I have many answered prayers: My son has moved into his new home. My daughter's multiple sclerosis does not keep her from working, studying for a doctorate, and volunteering to help others. My husband and I are aging, but still enjoying one another after many years of marriage. Amen.

- Confess your sins of commission and omission.

   I write: Gracious God, I confess my sin of omission when I did not fully explain the peace and calm that you have brought into my heart and soul. Help me to stand up with your word in trying to explain what is right. The Bible clearly says to request a pardon for our sins whether they are intentional or not. As I reflect on sins of commission from yesterday, I remember some specific words I spoke that were unnecessary. Forgive me for trespassing as I forgive others. Amen.

- Note when you spoke to someone about God.

   I write: My God, when Joyce learned that she would be able to acquire space in a first-class location downtown along the riverfront, we were thrilled. I was pleased that my books lived in her bookstore, but to move to such a prime location was like a miracle. After she met with the manager of the space, we were thrilled with his interest in her bookstore. She told me the deal was done. I told her we needed to thank God. We agreed in prayer. Amen.

The Bible Speaks to Writing

There are more than sixty-two verses in the Bible that address writing in some fashion. However, the three verses below speak especially to writing as it could be done in a journal:

- Luke 1:3–4

   Luke, a physician, is writing to encourage healing of any kind.

   "Therefore, since I myself have carefully investigated everything from the beginning, it seemed good also to me to write an orderly account for you, most excellent

Theophilus, so that you may know the certainty of the things you have been taught."

Here Luke is writing the results of his research to Theophilus. It is like a letter filled with good information that validates a truth.

- Deuteronomy 31:24

Moses is writing about Israel's rebellion being predicted.

"After Moses finished writing in a book the words of this law from beginning to end."

This represents Moses' completion of the writing of the book, as in "The End." After completing a journal with a specific purpose or story, it is helpful to note the end by summing it up in some way.

- Joshua 24:26

Joshua is telling the people to serve the Lord.

"And Joshua recorded these things in the Book of the Law of God. Then he took a large stone and set it up there under the oak near the holy place of the LORD."

This writing was part of a covenant whereby in a public act the words were witnessed. Such journal writing might represent a ceremony that may contain specific memorabilia.

Write Your Prayer

The point of my journaling is to write my prayer so that it becomes a part of me. It is my daily, thought-provoking worship. I read, write, think, reflect, and engage God. Because I have written my conversations with him, I have an opportunity to reread them.

How long do I write? When I first started, I wrote for an hour. Now it takes me thirty to forty-five minutes, depending on what I have to say to him about me or my loved ones or even the world, and what he has to say to me in return. I listen.

I use an outline of the Christian liturgical year of seasons in the church that determine times for celebration and observation. I follow the major liturgical periods of time: January starts another year until Easter or the Resurrection; Easter until Pentecost in May; and June through November, which is part of Ordinary Time (those periods that fall outside the major ceremonial seasons); and all of December, which is the season when we celebrate Jesus' birth. I support the purpose of the liturgical calendar as being to praise and worship Jesus from his birth to his incarnation, and ultimately to his ascension to heaven.

Prayer Outline and Prompt Phrases:

1. Mantra—Come to me Lord Jesus, send me your spirit. Create in me a clean heart. Create in me a forgiving spirit. _____.

2. I love you Lord, for you heard my voice and you heard my cry for mercy and responded by _____.

3. With gratitude I come before you, saying _____.

4. In closing, I ask _____.

Assignment

Above is one example of an outline with prompt phrases:

- Use the prompt phrases for three days in a row.
- Adapt the prompt phrases to reflect your style.
- Use your new prompt words for three more days.
- Make notes on what you learned about yourself, your writing, and your prayer.

My Prayer Examples

1. Mantra—Come to me Lord Jesus, send me your spirit. Create in me a clean heart. Create in me a forgiving spirit. *When*

things of the past come to me and I feel regretful, help me to let them go and move on.

2. I love you, Lord, for you heard my voice and you heard my cry for mercy and responded by *allowing me to participate in the homegoing service for a dear friend and joining with others to remember her as a fine person who gave of herself to others. I pray that her children are successful and as kind and sweet as she was.*

3. With gratitude, I come before you saying *thank you for my dear friends with whom I went to a fine restaurant and enjoyed an extraordinary evening of fellowship.*

4. In closing, I ask *you to show me how to help others.*

Chapter 5—Meditative Journaling

"Do not let this Book of the Law depart from your mouth;
meditate on it day and night, so that you may be
careful to do everything written in it. Then you will
be prosperous and successful."

JOSHUA 1:8

Prayer: Heavenly Father. I prayerfully meditate over your word as I try to become fully knowledgeable about your laws. Guide me so I can grow in wisdom according to your teachings. Thank you for your promise of success. Amen.

Spiritual Meditation Traditions

CHRISTIANITY, HINDUISM, BUDDHISM, JUDAISM, AND ISLAM represent the five major world religions. All include meditation as part of their rituals.

Worldwide in religious traditions, meditation is usually practiced with the purpose of transcending the mind and attaining enlightenment. Islamic meditation reaches for a sense of well-being and comfort in the present. Daoism, the Chinese philosophy and religion emphasizes living in harmony with nature.

There are other types of meditation, most of which stem from one of the above-mentioned religions. However, some commonly practiced ones include:

- Yoga means "union." It dates back to about 1700 BC and is the oldest and most widely practiced form of meditation. It is practiced in many forms that include breathing and body postures or poses.

- Transcendental meditation is a specific form of mantra meditation introduced in 1955, and was most popular in the 1960s and 1970s.

- Self-enquiry is the English translation for the Sanskrit term *atma vichara*. It means to ask, "Who am I?" to find your true self.

We are focusing on Christian meditation. The goal of Christian meditation is to communicate with God while ascertaining a more profound understanding of the Bible in order to grasp the word of God. We ask, "May my meditation be pleasing to him, as I rejoice in the LORD" (Ps 104:34).

Writing–Journaling

We have been identifying steps that are necessary to get ready to journal, things that are to be remembered or examined to chart the next course. If you think about it, we began this kind of writing during high school with many answers to questions that ask "What have you been doing with your life?" up to now. Then there was the college application that asked questions whose answers were supposed to enlighten the decision makers. Then we lived out our adult lives writing resumes for myriad reasons. They built upon one another. We've been writing about ourselves for a long time. At some point, like now, we realize we need to write it down for the sake of remembering, transitioning, or questioning.

When things are going smoothly and you get comfortable, life moves and things happen. Then the time comes to face difficult issues. Some of these prompts hold words that may help you start a meditative journal conversation with God.

Prompts

- Mourning the loss of a spouse. Can I find peace?

- We are empty-nesters. Our children are grown and gone. What now?

- I have a life-threatening disease. How can I get through this? Can I accept the ending?

- Where should I go: to a new city, or just down-size to an apartment?

- I'm retired with money and time to do what I want. What do I want to do?

- My job has ended and I want to do something on my own. What shall I do?

- I'm pregnant. What am I going to do with a baby without a husband?

- My daughter is having a baby. How can I parent an adult and be a grandparent?

- I don't want to sit at home alone. How can I find a job that pays?

You may be able to relate to these prompts. What do you want to remember or process? What monumental changes are you going through? Now let's move to meditative journaling by focusing on any one of the above prompts to jumpstart your writing in a quiet, peaceful environment.

Meditation

In this book, we are using meditation as a way to spend time in quiet thought for religious purposes or relaxation. Writing in a journal forces you to examine all aspects of the subject on your mind as you daydream about bettering the situation or rewriting the same thoughts again and again, deliberately examining the negativity to the point that it is understandable, or not. Such pondering gets you to the next level of willingness and ability to move on.

The word "meditate" comes from the Latin noun of action from the past participle stem of the word *meditāri*, which means to meditate, think over, reflect on, consider, study, plan, devise, rehearse, and practice. The root word "med" means to measure, limit, consider, advise, and take appropriate measures.

Given the Latin derivation of the word, our working definition of "journaling" will be: to write reflections on specific subjects in order to help devise a plan to take appropriate measures to help take hold of our lives.

In chapter 4, we used spiritual journaling as a reflection on the past, an examination of the now, and a look toward the future. It was a conversation with God.

Here we will use meditation as a form of journaling prayers to reach a thoughtful communication that takes us to a higher level of awareness with God.

"Meditate" and "meditation" are used more than twenty times in the Bible. In all cases, it means to ponder or contemplate or focus on something specific. Here are several examples:

- Psalm 1:2—". . . but whose delight is in the law of the Lord, and who meditates on his law day and night."

- Psalm 49:3—"My mouth will speak words of wisdom; the meditation of my heart will give you understanding."

- Psalm 119:99—"I have more insight than all my teachers, for I meditate on your statutes."

As shown in these Scriptures, the Bible tells us to think about God's word. Our thoughts control our behavior, therefore, what we think about and thus write about should help us get a hold of our life by journaling. God wants us to think about his word and meditate on it.

In *Satisfy Your Soul*, Dr. Bruce Demarest writes:

> A quieted heart is our best preparation for all this work of God...Meditation refocuses us from ourselves and from the world so that we reflect on God's Word, His nature, His abilities, and His works...So we prayerfully ponder, muse, and "chew" the words of Scripture. The goal is simply to permit the Holy Spirit to activate the life-giving Word of God.[1]

How Do You Do it?

Using a tape recorder, your smartphone, or pen and paper, find a quiet place to meditate by journaling. As often as you pray each day, you should meditate. Morning, noon, and night are always good prayer times. Upon waking in the morning and before falling asleep at night are common times. If you can fit a mid-day journaling in, that's perfect.

If there is something on your mind or you're working on issues to help get hold of your life, start there. If not, follow Philippians 4:8 and focus on "whatever is true, whatever is noble, whatever is right, whatever is pure, whatever is lovely, whatever is admirable—if anything is excellent or praiseworthy—think about such things."

Meditation and prayer are universally accepted as part of worship in most religions. Both are ways to be silent and still and alone. We pray to communicate with God. We meditate to communicate with ourselves. As you write your meditations, your thoughts are concentrated on your momentous journey, whether it be strategies to get hold of your life, dreams of the future, or unresolved issues. As you meditate, the environment that surrounds you encourages thoughts of how to relax in a calm and peaceful time.

---

1. Bruce Demarest, *Satisfy Your Soul: Restoring the Heart of Christian Spirituality* (Colorado Springs, CO: NAVPress, 1999), 133.

Journaling your meditation can also help you rediscover or reconnect with your prayer life. So often, we pray silently within our heads and have no way to keep our attention focused. Journaling overcomes all weaknesses in your prayer life. By writing your meditations, the depth goes deeper than the relaxation, which is often thought to be a result of meditation. Engaging in a practice of meditation produces a powerfully relevant way to pray that is rooted in mental concentration.

When we are stressed, we pray. We call on God. Meditative journaling about whatever is stressing you out can reduce stress. Calm yourself, focus, and write. It is effortless and leads to a new level of awareness that neutralizes the stress. Such meditative journaling helps you focus on the present moment and lessens the likelihood of your mind wandering.

Meditation can be solitary or communal. Meditating in groups helps you maintain a regular practice and allows you to connect with others who meditate. Rarely do groups write and meditate, but it is the discipline rather than the strategy. Writing frequently and on a schedule allows you to grow and get better, thereby gaining experience, which is the teacher that amplifies your alertness and effectiveness in meditative journaling. We write our meditations to keep our attention off things we don't want to address, and to nourish what we want to spotlight, especially when we're trying to get hold of our lives and make changes.

Rick Warren, in *The Purpose Driven Life*, describes Christian meditation this way: "Meditation is *focused* thinking. It takes serious effort. You select a verse and reflect on it over and over in your mind...if you know how to worry, you already know how to meditate."[2] Warren goes on to say,

> No other habit can do more to transform your life and make you more like Jesus than a daily reflection on Scripture . . . If you look up all the times God speaks about meditation in the Bible, you will be amazed at the

2. Rick Warren, *The Purpose Driven Life: What on Earth am I Here for?* (Grand Rapids: Zondervan, 2002), 190.

benefits He has promised to those who take the time to reflect on His Word throughout the day.[3]

Journal Meditation with Spiritual Mantras

All disciplines have a language. When Christians think about prayer, one of the first things that comes to mind is the Lord's Prayer, which gives clear guidance on exactly what to say. When we think of meditation, certain words come to mind such as breathing, sounds, body movements, and body poses. They relate to moving meditation, like yoga. As we add spiritual meditation to it, we expand the language purpose to include a vocabulary full of spiritually related words.

One folder on my personal computer that holds my spiritual journaling is titled "Meditative Prayers." I thought I created this combination of words for my personal use. Not so. Google "meditative prayers" and there are 465,000 results. In the early works of Robert Browning, it explains, "Both Eastern and Western Christian teachings have emphasized the use of meditative prayers as an element in increasing one's knowledge of Christ."[4]

In scanning the content of my folders, I discovered words that create prompts and questions for combining the discipline of meditation with prayer and spirituality. Here are but twenty:

1. Prayer—What is my favorite prayer strategy?
2. Answers—What was my last answered prayer?
3. Victory—How can I validate a victory?
4. Praise—How often should I praise God?
5. Love—How will I know whom to love?
6. Gifts—When shall I use the gifts of the Spirit?
7. Blessed—When will I know that I'm blessed?

3. Warren, *Purpose Driven Life*, 190.

4. Robert Browning, *The Byzantine Empire*, rev. ed. (Washington, DC: The Catholic University of America Press, 1992), 238.

8. Revelation—What revelation am I waiting for?

9. Devotion—What act of devotion pleases me most?

10. Promise—What promises in the Bible do I relate to?

11. God's will—How will I know it is God's will?

12. Thanksgiving—When should I say thank you?

13. Witness—When will I know it's time to witness?

14. Struggle—What is my most dominant struggle at this time?

15. Insight—Am I wise enough to understand my spiritual needs?

16. Spiritual—Am I able to discern meanings when I read the Bible?

17. Confession of sin—Am I clear about God's disappointment in my actions?

18. Lessons—Am I sure about what I am supposed to be doing?

19. Holy Spirit—How shall I let the Holy Spirit lead my life?

20. Mountaintop—When I get to the mountaintop, will I know it?

The lead words are so familiar in the spiritual world, yet we often don't analyze them despite the fact that they possess unique meanings that bring forth special feelings. Using the questions as prompts to begin journaling meditation may allow your mind to expand into something new. When the new thought comes forth, put your words in a sentence that may help you get hold of your life. Meditate on it by repeating it over and over until it opens your mind far beyond your expectations. Try it!

Meditation Environment

As one can pray anywhere, one should be able to meditate anywhere, thus, together, everywhere.

When we first think of meditating, we think of sitting still in a peaceful place that lends itself to quiet thinking, with few distractions. As we continue to meditate, we grow and realize that we can meditate in any environment.

Putting prayer and meditation together mandates place and space and tools to work with. With pen and pencil in hand, or a recorder, a special place is required. Perhaps you don't have a full prayer room, but find enough space where you can sit and be quiet. Look around your environment. There may be space in a closet, in the laundry room, in the bathroom, in the guest room, in the living room where no one goes to sit, at the piano that no one plays, on the porch or the patio, in the car. Go where you can meditate and pray in secret with no one else present. I journal on my personal computer at my desk in my private workroom, where I am alone.

Once you find the right place, here are ways to make sure your space is safe-meditative-prayer-ready.

- Safe place—Where no one can come upon you abruptly and frighten you or hurt you.

- Quiet place—Where the sounds of voices, unwanted music, or other electronic devices cannot disturb you.

- Unshared place—Where no one can join you to chat or socialize.

- Appealing space—Where you open your eyes and adore what you see.

Consecrate your space by calling on God to bless it and letting him know that you desire to make meditative prayer a disciplined practice.

Additionally, some outdoor spaces are refreshing, if you can concentrate given the surroundings. Returning to the same space as part of your routine helps reinforce your discipline and desire to continue for a consistent length of time. More than likely you will develop a ritual of getting yourself into your favorite position, reading Scripture, and meditating on the Scripture or an issue on your mind. This helps set the tone to ensure the time is fruitful and creative.

Since you have your journaling instruments in hand, you can document why you're meditating. Whether it is continuing a dialogue or creating a new dream, deciding at the beginning of your meditative prayer helps you focus and concentrate.

In your room, when you close the door, you close out the world and it's your time to engage in your meditative prayer. The beauty of journaling prayers is to write down the questions and answers when they come. "I call on you, my God, for you will answer me; turn your ear to me and hear my prayer" (Ps 17:6).

Compassion Meditation

Compassion meditation has become quite popular as a feel-good meditative strategy. It comes from Buddhists, who use it to open up their hearts and minds to become more compassionate.

When our feelings generate negative suggestions toward ourselves and others, it's time for compassion meditation to turn us around. The negativity needs to be let go of and dropped. But how? Perhaps praying repetitious phrases will help change the mood, words like the gifts of the Holy Spirit:

Thank you for the gifts of the Holy Spirit. Help me to repeat them now to create in me a clean heart filled with confidence.

- Love
- Joy
- Peace
- Patience
- Kindness
- Goodness
- Faithfulness
- Gentleness
- Self-control

Now that I have repeated them over and over, help me to slow down my repetition to recognize the meaning of each one. I must move to loving kindness and appreciative joy of myself before I can begin to have compassion for the one causing the negativity. I want to see the goodwill myself. If I can do this, I will understand that my heart chooses not to engage in seeing the negative side of that person as he does not realize that I am even staring at him.

When your heart feels different, as if for an unfamiliar or unpleasant person, this is the time to meditate in a similar manner. However, prayer may be needed to get you in the spirit. Even though you breathe the same and visualize the same, the tenderness is not the same.

Compassion forces you to think of your enemy and their suffering, yet it's imperative to revisit the peaceful times you had together as well, even though it's hard to wish them well as only you can hear your meditative prayer. As Galatians 6:10 reminds us:

> Therefore, as we have the opportunity, let us do good to
> all people, especially to those who belong to the family
> of believers.

Compassion is like doing good. It encompasses good things like kindness, concern, caring, and empathy. If we can imagine that our prayer meditation room is filled with compassion for us, we can express that same compassion to others.

Frequently, we get opportunities to do good to others. Usually, it happens spontaneously. We only feel the need for it when we discover negativity in our hearts. Then we call on compassion meditation to let go of that feeling and help us show loving-kindness.

It's easy to show compassion to those we love; just seeing them brings us joy. Should they become ill, we feel their suffering and pray for healing. Likewise, when we become ill, we pray for our healing. We express the same chants: Heal him. Heal me. God of Mercy. Heal him. Heal me.

Loving-kindness is also seen as a meditation practice. It has the attributes of love, such as friendliness and joy, that become components of compassion as you continue to practice while learning from the Father of compassion. We need caring as a tool to help change our lives. As 2 Corinthians 1:3–4 says:

> Praise be to the God and Father of our Lord Jesus Christ, the Father of compassion and the God of all comfort, who comforts us in all our troubles, so that we can comfort those in any trouble with the comfort we ourselves receive from God.

Assignment

- Find a word or phrase that lends itself to your meditative prayer.
- Write a meditative prayer or praise.
- Write a meditative prayer request.

Chapter 6—Journaling that Leads to Greatness

"The Lord your God is with you, he is mighty to save.
He will take great delight in you, he will quiet you
with his love, he will rejoice over you with singing."

ZEPHANIAH 3:17

Prayer: Heavenly Father, I want you to take great delight in me as I write daily in my journal, even when I don't acknowledge that you are with me. Remind me of your everlasting love and your unwillingness to be separated from me. Thank you for rejoicing with me. Amen.

IT'S ASTONISHING THAT SOME people reach greatness based on their talent, while other truly great people work hard like the rest of us, and yet never reach that pinnacle. Life's a long journey and greatness can be reached late in life, even when we think our life is near the end. While dreams may differ, the process of journaling toward them is the same. Here are a few great ones who switched careers after age FIFTY and became quite successful.

- President Ronald Reagan was an actor before his election to his first political office at age fifty-five. He became Governor of California in 1966, and U.S. President in 1981 at the age of sixty-nine. He served two presidential terms and ended his two terms at age seventy-seven. He was the oldest President at that time.

- Harland Sanders owned a restaurant and hotel before he became "the Colonel" and began selling Kentucky Fried Chicken franchises at age sixty-five.

- Laura Ingalls Wilder was a teacher before she published her first novel, at age sixty-five. The *"Little House on the Prairie"* series is world-famous. She published twelve additional children's books.

- Tim and Nina Zagat, husband and wife, were both corporate lawyers before they began printing their restaurant survey guide, "Zagat." In 2011, Google bought Zagat for $151 million. They were both seventy-one at the time of the sale.

- Bhakti Vedanta Swami Prabhupada was a chemist and Sanskrit scholar before he founded the Hare Krishna movement at age sixty-nine. He was spreading the teachings of Lord Krishna, an Indian divinity. Millions of people worldwide now follow the movement.

AARP Magazine qualifies the following individuals as being age-defying. The way they maintain their good looks seems effortless. It's not all in their genes. I believe they eat well and exercise often and remain positive. They are in their fifties, but still look good enough to medicate sore eyes:

Garth Brooks	Ellen DeGeneres
Janet Jackson	Marc Jacobs
Jon Bon Jovi	Michelle Obama
Michelle Pfeiffer	Brad Pitt
Russell Simmons	Blair Underwood

Changing careers after age fifty or after retirement is an anxiety-producing challenge. The thought of it generates fear beyond belief, but the truth may be that you've been dreaming about it since you were a child. In your dream, one day you would step on the stage and receive an award for your outstanding performance as an athlete, entertainer, inventor, manager, musician, professional, scientist, writer, owner, or for otherwise being the first person to accomplish something special.

With pen and journal in hand, let's begin. I answered the following questions and used them as prompts to initiate the dialogue to validate my dream.

- When I was a child, what did I want to do when I grew up? *I wanted to be a lawyer, because I thought lawyers sat at big desks and helped people with their problems.*

- What was my most vivid dream about doing something special? *I was in a national oratorical contest and I dreamed of being the winner and everyone in the audience applauding for me and the prize was a substantial scholarship. (I placed third and got a small scholarship.)*

- When I stand in front of the mirror and recite my acceptance speech, what is it for? *It is for a Pulitzer Prize.*

- The thought of being "what" gets me emotional? *Being the author of a New York Times bestselling book.*

- When I'm getting dressed in my favorite attire, what am I about to do? *Go to a dinner-dance fundraiser with friends.*

- How do I envision me at my physical best and what am I doing? *After my annual check-up, everything in my body is functioning all right. I take a five-mile walk.*

- When I am daydreaming, what am I imagining I am doing? *Being a guest speaker at a spiritual event with the opportunity to sell my books.*

- When an accomplishment is magnificent, excellent, and results in happiness for me, what is next? *My reward is traveling to a place where there is water, fine restaurants, and an opportunity to have a new experience.*

- What is the most exciting thing I want to accomplish before my demise? *I want to take an extraordinary vacation with my children and their families.*

- What is your bucket list of ten things that you've not done, but want to do?

  1. *Be a woman in whom the Holy Spirit chooses to dwell.*

  2. *See our daughter healed of multiple sclerosis.*

  3. *Attend our daughter's wedding.*

  4. *Attend our son's wedding.*

  5. *Travel across the country promoting my spiritual book on journaling.*

  6. *Publish a New Testament book of prayers.*

  7. *Publish a book about the promises in Proverbs.*

  8. *Publish twenty-five spiritual books and novels.*

  9. *Purchase a vacation home on an island in the Caribbean.*

  10. *Take my two aunts (ages eighty-one and eighty-six) on an extraordinary vacation.*

We've answered the questions and written far more than we thought we had to say. We may have identified the emotional core of the dream. It's clear we know exactly what we want to do.

Now, write a summation of the dreamed undertaking in one sentence. Mine is: *I want to be an award-winning writer who travels around the world promoting journaling as a way to take hold of your life.* What say you? "What we will be has not yet been made known" (John 3:2).

At the end of a Visioning Retreat session of seven women who possess lofty aspirations, I wrote this prayer to state my position and desire for my participation in the group as one who is looking to become someone special:

> *Dear Lord, thank you for letting me know that my dream will come true. When it comes true, I can and will help those I want to help or you will do it for me. Keep me*

*committed to the victims whom I have hurt. Thank you
for the calm I feel, knowing and trusting in you that my
dreams will come true and my prayers will be answered.
I believe I'm going to soar across the country and speak to
strangers about you with my book on journaling.*

*I want to be ready. No. Direct me. Teach me. Show me
how to be ready for my next engagement. Give me the tools
I need to deal with the issues in front of me.*

Thank you for what you've done for me as I feel physically and spiritually fit.

*Thank you for these ladies who have come into my
life. Help us all to grow together as our dreams come true
and we depart from one another. Amen.*

What is Journaling Helping Me to Accomplish?

The more I wrote and reviewed my writing, my thoughts became more aligned with my dreams. I did not feel guilty about the necessary components of my dream, such as the need for money and the search for a publisher and buy-in from my husband. I realized the need for a business and marketing plan that spells excellence and not mediocrity.

Every day I wrote, it became clearer and clearer that I was sitting in silence with God, journaling my most intimate thoughts and feelings. My writings forced me to focus on my finances and write about how I spend money. I wrote about my friends, family members, and associates who crossed a path in my dream. I had to make sure they continued to fit in my life, or not. It became clear that I must grow in grace with the mercy of God at my back.

Journaling is helping me achieve a viewing of the seasons and the timing of God's lessons. "You will pray to him, and he will hear you, and you will fulfill your vows" (Job 22:27).

Some days in my journaling, I realize the need to say thank you for something I had not asked for. It's like his whisper saying "I am here by your side." Last week, I was with my doctor, who was running late, which caused me to be late for a consulting appointment. I was nervous and upset because it is unacceptable to be late when you've had plenty of time to reschedule one appointment or the other. I called the client to say that I was going to be late. The client asked, "Didn't you receive my message? We cannot make it today, we will have to reschedule."

God had my back.

The reminder that God is omnipresent took me to a new level in my journaling as I try to reach greatness. It is now time to write forward, listing the steps I need to take and how to take them, remembering that God is at my side and he is all-powerful.

Mapping the Dream

Creating the life we want requires that we distinguish between what is necessary to reach the highest level of our dream, and what is not. Then we must make sure that our dream is not just for us, but for the higher good, and that it reaches others and provides some help to them.

Before we begin to map our dream, we must identify the people, places, and experiences that influence our lives. This list creates the framework in which to explore different factors that have been a part of our past and those we need in the future.

My life map concept begins with a circle. Outside the circle are all the people I want to encourage to use journaling to take hold of their lives by carefully figuring out how to make their dreams come true. Inside the circle are all the things I need to do to reach my dream. I give each one ten degrees. Then, inside that ten degrees, I list five steps I need in order to achieve my desired goal. For example, in order to effectively target senior audiences who may want to take hold of their lives, I would do the following things:

1. *Contact senior housing communities and ask to present my journaling book.*

2. *Volunteer as a speaker for AARP in exchange for selling my journaling book.*

3. *Moderate at university retirement classes to promote my journaling book.*

4. *Ask churches and senior communities to put my journaling book in their libraries.*

5. *Ask hospitals to make my book available in their gift shops.*

Although my example focuses on marketing, there are other issues in the circle, such as writing a book, finding a publisher and agent, ordering books, funding travels, setting up the sales transactions, developing a business plan, creating a short-term and long-term budget, and determining my legal needs. Each action has at least five steps that are necessary to accomplish the task.

The complete inner circle concept represents the To-Do Lists for my dream. The vision came when I discovered authors who reveal life-changing events that can help make their readers' dreams come true. Most self-help books tell you some things to do. In my book here, I say journaling about today can be comforting, but being open to tomorrow can be exciting. In my dream, I want to tell the world that journaling can help you take hold of your life and subsequently, you'll be happy. "Commit to the LORD whatever you do, and he will establish your plans" (Prov 16:3).

Writing the Dream

When I meditate without writing, I may fall asleep or my mind may drift around different subjects. I daydream about reaching the pinnacle of my life every now and then, but in minutes my mind shifts to my environment, a sound, tomorrow's dinner, my friend's birthday party, etc.

Writing my greatness dream in explicit detail helps me to observe myself in a different way, in a different place, with people applauding and praising me for my talent. It's exciting to think about a special event in my dream, but it takes too long to describe every aspect of it in writing. But I must start in a slow, methodical manner, describing the surroundings. I must connect with the insight

I'm getting from my inner thoughts. As I reread my writings, I generate new thoughts which go in a variety of directions.

I'm clear about what I want to do, but how do I chart my success? My mapping is done. I must determine my shortcomings that keep me from reaching greatness.

You must practice in order to be like the best. In my case, I need to write more and give more speeches. I must practice. It's like the piano. In order to play well, I must practice daily. It's not like riding a bicycle. Once you learn to ride, you have one more added skill you won't forget, like writing your name, typing without looking, counting to 100, saying your ABCs, or driving a car.

I'm committed to writing four hours each day to hone my skill. I write each day in my prayer journal to commune with God. In my dream journal, I write about any progress in my life's plan in an effort to make sure I understand what else I should be doing to improve my talent so that I can achieve my dream. In addition to writing, my To-Do List demands that I take specific action. As I sit here writing now, I know I must slow down and do something to get me to my greatness. I am doing something. I am writing. But maybe I need a role model. I want to watch someone great at work to motivate me to reach up to be the best.

My role model is meticulous, she keeps a performance journal to assess her daily activities, to correct her mistakes, and to track her progress. In my journal, I reflect and write about what I want to do. I have a photo of my role model and I look at her every day because her photo is on the back of my closet door where I hang my nightclothes. Each day, when I stare at her, I get a courageous feeling of superiority as I know I can do what she does and do it better.

I am going to watch a movie about her life story. What was she like? She testified before Congress and is now an international advocate for imprisoned women. At one point in her life, she went to prison and became renewed as she repented and became a renowned speaker and an award-winning writer. She led a movement, people followed, and she won awards. I want to be her.

It takes a plethora of complex experiences to become great and it takes a good storyteller to write the story about it. Men have become great and their lives have changed generations, and then they have written about it. They became great because they faced obstacles, dreamed of making some part of life better for others, and made money traveling the world sharing their stories. Nelson Mandela wrote *A Long Walk to Freedom* after twenty-five years in prison for starting a movement. Mahatma Gandhi wrote of his life while living *The Story of My Experiments with Truth*. Angela Davis wrote *The Meaning of Freedom and Other Difficult Decisions* after a time in prison during the Civil Rights movement in the 1960s.

I want to liken myself to these people with my dream to help people take hold of their lives by journaling. I've faced the obstacle of serving time in prison. I also have a strategy to share, though perhaps it is not as great as theirs.

Like Martha Stewart, Malcolm X, Charles Colson, Rev. Martin Luther King, Jr., a prison term changed my life and gave me a new vision and a clear method to share with people who want to take hold of their lives. My change came from having time to reflect and rebuild my mind and recalculate my senses.

Most importantly, I believe God has forgiven me of my wrong and given me a signal that the path is clear for me to write forward. I believe God forgave me, just as he does anyone who asks, such as King David, a favored king in the Bible. Jesus is in his lineage. Even though he murdered Bathsheba's husband in order to be with her, he repented. God forgave him, and he became one of Israel's greatest kings and a creative writer in the book of Psalms. Together, he and Bathsheba bore a son who became the great king Solomon. Then, David asked for forgiveness in Psalm 51:10–13.

> Create in me a pure heart, O God,
>   and renew a steadfast spirit within me.
> Do not cast me from your presence
>   or take your Holy Spirit from me.
> Restore to me the joy of your salvation
>   and grant me a willing spirit, to sustain me.

> Then I will teach transgressors your ways,
> so that sinners will turn back to you.

Some of us will reach greatness and some won't, but I want to give it a try. In my greatness journal, my first sentence is: I want to be great because I would like to embrace people who want to take hold of their lives, and to help them journal their way during the journey to reach their goals. I think if I work hard and endeavor to reach a level of excellence, I can get there. But I must live my life by pursuing my "Prophecy of Ps": passion, practice, prowess, presence, perseverance, and permission to succeed. "But test them all; hold on to what is good, reject every kind of evil" (1 Thess 5:21–22).

Assignment

- In one sentence, select a few words that describe what you want to be, such as "great," "well-known," "famous," "celebrated," "notable," "ordinary," etc.

- In two sentences, explain the reason for your depiction.

Chapter 7—Writing Your Memoir

"Truly I tell you, wherever this gospel is preached throughout
the world, what she has done will also be told, in memory of her."

MATTHEW 26:13

Prayer: Heavenly Father, I want to be remembered
for doing some good. Show me how to say something
so extraordinary in my writings that others will want
to remember. Thank you for giving me a lifetime of
memories that may be helpful when someone reads
them. Amen.

L IFE CHANGES MAY BRING about the need or desire to write a
memoir, or perhaps testify as to how you got through with
God's help. The loss of a spouse might make you want to write
about all the good times and the most essential decisions you
made together. An empty nest filled with quiet is perfect for writing about the times you want your children to remember most.
Grandchildren are often deeply interested in stories about their
parents and other family members.

Unlike an autobiography, which may encompass a whole
life, a memoir captures only those memories you want to share
with others, much like a testimony that presents a part of your
life where you followed the word of God. It is a slice of your life.
For instance, Bill Clinton wrote a memoir on his experience as

President of the United States. There are many aspects of his life he could have chosen to write about, but his presidency was the segment he chose to focus on.

Memoir, Autobiography, and Biography

A memoir usually covers a special portion of one's life that readers outside your world can put into context with the environment or a historical event. It reflects your personal knowledge and experiences.

An autobiography covers the author's entire life to the present and includes details that are not public and only known by the author.

A biography is written by an author who has researched the happenings in someone else's life.

Examples of Memoirs

I would suggest you read one of these or any other well-known memoir.

The Diary of a Young Girl—Anne Frank

The Diary of a Young Girl (also known as "The Diary of Anne Frank.") stems from a diary kept by Anne Frank while she was in hiding for two years with her family during the Nazi occupation of the Netherlands.

The family was apprehended in 1944, and Anne Frank died of typhus in the Bergen-Belsen concentration camp. Her father, Otto Frank, was the only family survivor and he was given the diary, which has since been published in many adaptations and more than sixty different languages.

Night—Elie Wiesel

Eliezer "Elie" Wiesel, a Romanian-born Jewish writer, professor, political activist, and Nobel Laureate, authored fifty-seven books based on his experiences as a prisoner in the Auschwitz, Buna, and Buchenwald concentration camps. Wiesel died at age eighty-seven in 2016. His most famous book, *Night,* was on the *New York Times* bestseller list. More than 10 million copies were sold.

I Know Why the Caged Bird Sings—Maya Angelou

Maya Angelou (April 4, 1928—May 29, 2014) was born Marguerite Annie Johnson. Although Angelou was an author, poet, dancer, actress, and singer, her seven major books were autobiographies covering some aspect of her life. Her first book, *I Know Why the Caged Bird Sings,* tells of her life from age four to seventeen. Her last book, *Mom and Me,* recaptured her entire life, and included her mother as a key figure.

Eat, Pray, Love: One Woman's Search for Everything Across Italy, India and Indonesia—Elizabeth Gilbert

Gilbert goes on a journey with specific purposes: one country for the pleasure of the senses, another for spiritual enlightenment, and the third to restore balance in her life. The book becomes a travelogue, in which she learns to eat and enjoy new foods, learns to pray, and learns to love. Italy is full of Italian meals and she learns the language. In India, she spends four months in prayer and meditation and finds God. In Indonesia, she finds her love, whom she ultimately married.

Out of Africa—Karen Blixen

This memoir by the Danish author Baroness Karen von Blixen-Finecke was first published in 1937. It describes her seventeen years in Kenya and tells of her trials on her coffee plantation.

The 1985 film version starring Meryl Streep and Robert Redford is a love story—with myriad embellishments—based on two biographies of Blixen. Some of Blixen's more poetic narration and a few episodes from the book appear in the film, which won seven Academy Awards, including Best Picture, Best Director, and Best Screenplay Adaptation.

Orange Is the New Black: My Year in a Women's Prison (titled *Orange Is the New Black: My Time in a Women's Prison* in some editions)—Piper Kerman

In this memoir, Kerman tells the story of her time spent in a Connecticut prison camp for women and the money laundering and drug trafficking conviction that got her there. Two agents met with her in 1998, and six years later, she was sentenced to fifteen months in a federal prison camp for women. After serving time in three different facilities, Kerman was released in March 2005. *Orange is the New Black* is the basis of a Netflix award-winning television series.

Your Christian Testimony

A testimony is defined as a formal written or spoken statement, especially one given in a court of law. Here we will use testimony as written or spoken statements to recount a religious conversion or experience.

Christian testimonies are usually shared among Christians, and tell of how people came to know God along with specific experiences that include God's amazing intercession in their lives. There is always an expression of gratitude for something he has done to make some facet of their lives better.

As an example, my recent testimony included how he is helping me get through this difficult time of accepting my daughter's illness. Although I pray for complete healing, I continue to have faith in him as she gets up every day and handles all of the challenges of her life with grace. I can truly testify to the fact that, "The LORD is my rock, my fortress and my deliverer; my God is my rock, in whom I take refuge, my shield and the horn of my salvation, my stronghold" (Ps 18:2).

Here are a few of the many verses in the Bible which speak to the use of a testimony.

1 John 5:11—"And this is the testimony: God has given us eternal life, and this life is in his Son."

1 John 5:10—"Whoever believes in the Son of God accepts this testimony. Whoever does not believe God has made him out to be a liar, because they have not believed the testimony God has given about his Son."

John 15:26–27—"When the Advocate comes, whom I will send to you from the Father—the Spirit of truth who goes out from the Father—he will testify about me. And you also must testify, for you have been with me from the beginning."

Revelation 12:11—"They triumphed over him by the blood of the Lamb and by the word of their testimony; they did not love their lives so much as to shrink from death."

Revelation 19:10—"At this I fell at his feet to worship him. But he said to me, 'Don't do that! I am a fellow servant with you and with your brothers and sisters who hold to the testimony of Jesus. Worship God! For it is the Spirit of prophecy who bears testimony to Jesus.'"

Your Memoir Journal

Memoirs share the ups and downs of your life in hopes that a reader may learn from them. When you write about your life, you view situations through different lenses. Memoirs come in all shapes, colors, and sizes, just like people. They represent the ultimate tapestry of your life, or better yet, the legacy of your life. Daily journaling about past life events will help you generate content for your memoir. "I remember the days of long ago; I meditate on all your works and consider what your hands have done" (Ps 143:5).

Since it is your memoir journal, it's your story. You may write about any event of your life like sports, travel, family, childrearing, starting a company, or when your dog died. Journaling for your memoir may give you an opportunity to clear the air about some family secret, solve a longstanding problem, give folks a chance to apologize to you (or you to them), and testify to God's goodness in overwhelming situations.

You don't have to write your entire autobiography, just collect the earliest memories that redirected your life or mistakes, and which are worth sharing. Even though your story is a memoir, it must read like a good novel, with a narrative, plot, place, scene, and characters. And, your story must pass the test of being nonfictional so as to be called a memoir.

Writing about occurrences chronologically is not important. Simply begin with a memory that still renews a special feeling of a place in time or something from your journal.

As the narrator, you must present the issues from your heart that may help others remember you the way you want to be remembered. Perhaps, now you want them to know "that what has happened to me has actually served to advance the gospel" (Phil 1:12).

Your memoir is supposedly nonfiction. Publishers are squeamish about new writers and memoirs since James Frey published *A Million Little Pieces* as a memoir with fictional elements included. A memoir can employ reconstructed scenes and dialogue to dramatize the story. And it doesn't hurt to come out and say you've done so. In fact, these days most memoirs begin with an author's note stipulating that some names and events have been altered to protect people's privacy and for the sake of the story. But you cannot falsify events, such as the few hours in an Ohio police station that Frey turned into three months in prison. "Do your best to present yourself to God as one approved, a worker who does not need to be ashamed and who correctly handles the word of truth" (2 Tim 2:15).

Fact-check your memoir by reviewing your photo albums, notes from events, newspapers, and by talking to people who were involved in your life. Search for evidence that points to the situation. Check old newspapers to verify the events that were occurring at the same time. Don't rely on your memory. For example, if something happened on a particular street when you were age nine, you have your version of how that street looked; however, you may not remember enough details to engage readers, especially if some readers remember the 1950s better than you do. Your memory might be highly exaggerated. The word *novel,* after all, means "new," while memoir comes from "to remember."

Don't write about events that did not happen to you because a memoir is a documentation of events penned by you based on your familiarity with them. Writing about others' experiences from your point of view creates a novel, not a memoir. Your story requires a narrative with a beginning, middle, and end.

A memoir must be believable. By its very nature, the memoir says, "This *did* happen. This *can* happen." Tom Grimes, author of the memoir *Mentor,* included the story of his sister's suicide attempt. He says "I am trying to remember not only events and conversations but also emotions related to who I was, what occurred, and how I felt about what occurred."[1]

If you must write your story to remove the memories from your mind, everything you write will lead back to the same events. You want to make a point about your situation so that others may understand and align their past memories with yours. If you feel compelled to do so, write the unadorned truth as you remember it. "You will know the truth, and the truth will set you free" (John 8:32).

Write a chapter for your book as an essay or like a story you might read in your favorite magazine. Such an exercise may be a test of your style and contentment with your story. Allow others to read your story to determine if they are as moved by your experience as you were. After all, you wrote about it. Then decide to self-publish it or seek a publisher.

---

1. Tom Grimes, *Mentor: A Memoir* (Portland, OR: Tin House, 2010), 144.

Memoir: Fact or Fiction?

As I have said, a memoir should be true. The author should not alter reality when telling a story. Memories are flawed, but authors are expected to check facts and timelines to ensure accuracy.

Memoirs are usually written in first person by the author, and tell a specific story. It does not need to follow the author's entire life, but rather selected events that make up a unique scenario that only the author knows. Once the event is determined, then you must explain how it affected your life to the point that it would become interesting reading. Real-life experiences create stories that readers can relate to, as some have had similar experiences or perhaps knew someone who was impacted by such an occurrence. If the event changed your life or produced a new worldview for you, it is certainly worth writing about. It may influence how the readers see the same event, or a similar one, in their own lives.

Carefully choose your story characters. If members of your family, associates, or colleagues are included, it is imperative that you confer with them and include their view of the event, as it may differ from yours and require revising portions of the story. Because you are in control of writing your story, you don't want anyone to read it and say it's not true because they saw it differently than you did.

Research. Research. Research. Pull out all of your journals, diaries, photo albums, videos, and memorabilia, and ask your family and friends to go through theirs. As you assess all the mementos, the story may change.

Now that you've focused on your memoir on paper, it's time to explain what really happened to the point that you want the world to read about it. Or maybe this memoir is only meant for your children and grandchildren, to share with them the full account of a particular episode.

As you put together your outline, be honest with yourself. Even though you want to describe a series of events that led up to the main event, there must be a turning point that brings forth the final resolution. Be truthful, since "each of us will give an account of ourselves to God" (Rom 14:12).

The famous memoirs I mentioned earlier are important because they were honest stories about real-life experiences that readers can identify with. All of them included paragraphs of despair, humor and "a-ha" moments. If writing a memoir is too overwhelming, journal your daily thoughts about the process you're going through in preparing to write a memoir. Journal the changes in your thoughts about the event and the life changes which have occurred since that event took place. It will become an unexpected gathering of memories that may touch your heart or impact how you get hold of your life by journaling, and is useful preparation for memoir writing.

I've been thinking about writing my memoir. It's taking up some weighty space in my Daily Journal, in which I am trying to be anchored by staying alive and healthy and striving to succeed in my dreams.

I am assessing my progression by looking at what's good right now and looking forward. If I write my memoir, I believe that everything I write should be of service to someone. I want my life to be more than an exercise in comfort. When I write about my life, it must include a dissertation on my faith in God because I believe I have been endowed with the power to live with purpose. "For we are God's handiwork, created in Christ Jesus to do good works which God prepared in advance for us to do" (Eph 2:10).

ASSIGNMENT

- Write a mini-memoir (150 words or less).
- Describe the reasons for the event you have selected.
- Include a story arc—beginning, middle, and end.
- Conclude with one sentence that describes what you are telling readers to learn from your story.

Chapter 8–Take Control of Your Life by Journaling

"'Here comes that dreamer!' they said to each other."

GENESIS 37:19

Prayer: Heavenly Father, my dream is to be in your service and share your word in my writings. Transform my dream into a reality that pleases you. Thank you for allowing me to dream. Amen.

I BELIEVE YOU CAN TAKE control of your life by writing your way into a new place in a journal. My reason is based on the fact that my busy mind has a short attention span. As I think about something I want to do, it is usually so involved that I cannot keep the thought. I cannot pay attention to my thinking because my senses are distracting me. With pen and paper in hand, I can preserve my thoughts. If I can't think fast enough, I can audio tape my words to preserve them.

"I want to take control of my life and put it together again," is a frequently made statement. We assume our lives are in shambles, but if our life is a puzzle, the pieces are there, and we can fit them in place. If our life is a quilt, we can piece together the complex combination of things and make something beautiful and satisfying. Whether we liken our lives to a puzzle or a quilt, when we lay out the pieces, they're all in disarray. However, "we know that in all things God works for the good of those who love him, who have been called according to his purpose" (Rom 8:28).

So you want to put your life together again? Where was your life before? Where is your life this time? Where will your life be the next time?

The last time is in the past and I neither want to dwell on it nor repeat it, even though I learned from these experiences. This time is now and it represents a status report. The next time is in the future and that's where I want to go. Consider the questions below to create your answers that will guide you on your path. The answers which follow are mine. However, utilize your words in brief descriptions to get ready to move your life in another direction.

Use brief descriptions to shorten any anxiety that may be waiting to arise.

The last time . . . in the past . . .

1. When I was in school? *I was concerned about my appearance, grades, having friends, and being selected to be a part of school activities.*

2. When I was in church? *I was enjoying the fellowship and activities.*

3. When I was married? *I was excited about living with my soul mate, having children, cohabitating, and experiencing a new life with more family and friends.*

4. When I was divorced? *I was concerned about my emotions: heartache, feeling isolated, angry, deserted, and unhappy.*

5. When I had my first child? *I was young and pleased with every aspect of it, sex, birth, child-rearing, and providing grandchildren for my parents.*

6. When I felt imprisoned? *I was unhappy because of the regimentation, the lock-up, the lack of family present, and the incarcerated lifestyle.*

7. When my parents died? *I was unwilling to accept having no family, lonely holidays, no home-cooked food, and becoming an orphan.*

8. When I was first diagnosed with an illness? *I was down in the dumps, feeling disbelief, anger, loneliness, and fear.*

9. When I was stressed? *I was concerned about finances, spirituality, family, and work.*

10. When I retired? *I was pleased to have a steady income, an empty nest, a home, daytime activities, and travel opportunities.*

This time . . . now . . .

Presently, I must bring current the issues of the past, such as schooling, church affiliation, marriage, divorce, death of loved ones, illnesses, consistent stresses, and retirement. Given what I have journaled about in the past, it's now time to update each situation and either incinerate it, grow with it, or let it continue to be part of my daily life.

The next time . . . in my future . . .

Here are examples of my plans going forward:

1. School: *I shall only study topics that interest me. No more school.*

2. Church: *I shall pursue my faith as I am heaven-bound.*

3. Marriage: *I shall never marry again.*

4. Divorce: *I shall never divorce again.*

5. Children: *I hope to have grandchildren, someday.*

6. Imprisoned: *I shall never feel that way again.*

7. Death: *I look foward to seeing loved ones in heaven.*

8. Illness: *I shall begin my Life's End Journal.*

9. Stress: *I shall be at peace with myself.*

10. Retirement: *I shall move into a retirement community.*

As I reviewed my life's past and the present, I became aware of the need to have something greater than good feelings. I realized it might be time to think of, and plan for, a greater good. Based on where I've been and where I am, I believe the short time ahead can be awesome. Realizing that our names are written in heaven, the years ahead should be a joy ride. I am absolutely ready to grab on to the plan God has for me, along with the fruits of the Holy Spirit to help maneuver in our daily lives. "The fruit of the Spirit is love, joy, peace, forbearance, kindness, goodness, faithfulness, gentleness, and self-control" (Gal 5:22–23).

We all know about the apostle Paul. He was an unbeliever who became a believer, and he became a great man of God, all because he worked with the grace and power that God gave him through the Holy Spirit. When Paul went into the desert for three years, the Holy Spirit instructed him in God's ways.

It is believed that Paul learned how to be led and empowered by the Holy Spirit so he could fulfill all of his divine missions for the Lord. And we all have divine missions to fulfill. As Paul said, "May the grace of the Lord Jesus Christ, and the love of God, and the Communion of the Holy Spirit be with you all" (2 Cor 2:13–14).

That sounds like a powerful "go-forth" statement. He is telling us that we can make contact with the Holy Spirit, and once we make that contact with the Holy Spirit, then he will teach us how to be led and taught by him so we can then accomplish our divine destiny for him.

My Destiny

So, how can I determine my divine destiny? I scrolled through the Bible and found many familiar verses that encourage me to rely on his direction. Here are a several:

Philippians 4:13

"I can do all this through him who gives me strength."

Proverbs 16:9

"In their hearts humans plan their course, but the LORD establishes their steps."

Psalm 37:23

"The LORD makes firm the steps of the one who delights in him."

Psalm 37:4–5

"Take delight in the LORD, and he will give you the desires of your heart. Commit your way to the LORD; trust in him and he will do this."

I like Psalm 37:4–5 most of all. He promises me the desires of my heart. My desires are to help unbelievers become believers through my books and my speeches, to become closer to God, to pray continually, to read the words of the Lord, and to share with others the comfort I receive from God through journaling my prayers and meditations.

My Write Forward Journal includes the following sections to help me prepare to take hold of my life by journaling:

- Spiritual Desires—Remaining in Christ
- Book Writing—Notes for writing my next book
- Traveling—Locations I want to visit
- Meetings—Groups of people I want to meet, such as seniors, women's clubs, and junior high and high school students
- Finances—Savings plan to pay for my travels
- Wellness—Monitor my exercise regime and eating habits
- Outreach—List the people to whom I witness in any way
- Goodness—List my daily acts of goodness that helped someone

- Family—Host frequent get-togethers
- Friends—Keep in touch via telephone and gatherings.

With all of God's promised power, I believe I can take hold of my life by journaling and do anything. I will start by organizing my Write Forward Journal into specific sections. If I write daily and stay focused, a new and better me will evolve and I can live out the rest of my life in an astounding manner.

For the rest of my life, I will endeavor to reach out to people and discuss how writing can change their lives if they keep a journal that is marked up with spiritual thoughts.

Assignment

- To take control of your life by journaling, list the sections you need in your Write Forward Journal.

Chapter 9—Life's End Journal

"Therefore, I urge you, brothers and sisters,
in view of God's mercy, to offer your bodies as a living sacrifice,
holy and pleasing to God—this is your true and proper worship."

ROMANS 12:1

Prayer: Heavenly Father, as I prepare myself to end this life on earth, I want to write about my past and review it to ensure that I have traveled a path to the kingdom. Help me to take control of my life so that it becomes acceptable to you. Show me how to be a person in whom you are pleased to dwell. Amen.

A LIFE'S END JOURNAL IS a section in one of your journals that contains the final writings for others to read. As we said, one way to take hold of your life is to reflect on the past and map out some strategies for the future. You still have time. We will address the future in the next chapter.

In your Life's End Journal, write down all your thoughts relative to your final service, including thoughts on your eulogy, obituary, and epitaph. The questions become: What do you want your friends and family to say about you? What do you want the chatter to be when they learn new things about you? What do you want your legacy to be? What body of your work do you want your friends, family, and the public to know about? As frequently as you think on these subjects, write in this journal, noting the date, time, and place, as they may be important at some later date.

In my class of college-educated retired folk, my eagerness to introduce the need to write their own eulogy, obituary, and epitaph was not totally well received. Only 70 percent of the class was interested. In fact, two women did not come to this particular class discussion because they had no interest in the subject.

Their varying comments can be summed up as "I will be dead. It will make no difference to me." I believe they agree with Romans 14:8, which says, "If we live, we live for the Lord; and if we die, we die for the Lord. So, whether we live or die, we belong to the Lord." The majority of the class participants, however, engaged in the exercises and assignments. At least they now possess some notes about how they would like their families to proceed with life-ending services and memories. Even though we have many decisions to make about end-of-life issues, writing in a Life's End Journal can help with planning or sharing with a family member.

In my church, our services are seen as home-goings, as the deceased are going to their heavenly home to be with God. We celebrate the life with song and sermon, along with a repast for family and friends. Some funeral services have a casket, which is open or closed. Others are memorial services with only photos and flowers, usually held sometime after the death occurred.

Planning the Funeral

Before we start writing the eulogy, obituary, and epitaph, there are different types of funeral services to consider. In most cases, the culture and religion dictate the service. Most cultures possess specific customs related to such services. Religious services are usually held in a church or place of worship with customary liturgies.

No matter the culture or religion, three aspects are pertinent to the event: 1) A death has occurred, leaving a loss of one person; 2) a body must be disposed of, or put in a place where it will not disturb the living; and 3) a live person must make the arrangements.

If you want to have a say in your funeral service, there are some topics that should be considered when you consult a funeral home. It would help to jot down your thinking about each of the following issues in your Life's End Journal as they come to mind. This is not a journal you need to write in every day, only on those days when you're thinking about the subjects or some reminder comes forth.

Here are twenty thoughts to consider as sections in your Life's End Journal.

Paperwork

1. Put your will and other documents in order and designate someone to be in charge of them.

2. List family, friends, and other folks who will need to be notified.

3. Notify clubs and associations for special commemorations.

4. Set aside funds to pay for the service.

Writing

5. Create a press announcement.

6. Write letters to people whom you would like to have say something special.

7. Write random thoughts that come to mind.

Messages for Loved Ones

8. Say goodbye in some way to special people.

9. Select a charity for any donations, or accept flowers.

Funeral Planning

10. Decide on a public or private service.

11. Determine who should participate in the service.

12. Design a program with the order of service.

13. Draft the eulogy, obituary, and epitaph, as well as stories, poems, and other readings.

14. Describe the kind of service you would like to have, such as a memorial service, church service, or cultural service.

15. Locate a place for the service, such as a funeral home chapel, a religious place of worship, a cemetery chapel, a graveside, or a home.

16. Make a decision regarding the viewing (will it be an open or closed casket?) and social gathering.

17. Make a decision regarding what the post-funeral activities will be, such as the luncheon, repast, and/or family reception.

18. Plan the burial and grave location and the procession to the site.

19. Decide if you want to be buried, cremated, or sent to a research lab.

20. Choose a headstone or grave marker.

Eulogy, Obituary, and Epitaph

A eulogy is a commendatory oration or writing especially in honor of one deceased.

An obituary is a notice of a person's death usually with a short biographical account.

An epitaph is an inscription or brief statement on a tomb or gravestone in memory of the one buried there.

Eulogy

You may say you want others to write your eulogy, but wouldn't it be better if they had some words from you to work with? Eulogies include personal stories, songs, and poetry that remind your family and friends of you. This is a time to honor you and pay tribute to your life and your accomplishments. Celebrate the worthy parts of your life and your personality.

Before you determine if you want to write your eulogy or have someone else write it, these steps may help you begin collecting your thoughts:

- List in chronological order the most memorable events in your life.

- Look at your list and decide who should read it.

- Decide if you want the eulogy to be joyful or sad.

- End with a poem or song that uniquely describes you.

- Create an outline for someone else to use and present it to them or write your own.

My Eulogy

I don't write in my Life's End Journal every day, but I write when something reminds me of my demise. I once had an extraordinary hour filled with joy, the way it's defined in the Bible. In fact, during our weekly prayer call with my lady cousins and aunts, my daughter led a discussion on exploring the fruit of the spirit and focused on joy. When she finished, tears came to my eyes as I listened, on my cell phone, to her articulate the astounding aspects of joy.

In her recap, she said: "Joy results when we discover the presence, power, and purpose of God in every circumstance. Joy results from experiencing complete restoration and staying and remaining in God by receiving and obeying his word."

In her conclusion, she said: "People are searching for a joy which comes from the inside, and if you have it you can be sure people will be asking you how they can get it. . . . When someone asks the reason for the hope they observe in you, be ready to answer—God. May we be the people who not only know Christ but also find joy in him."

I've decided that I want my daughter to create and read my eulogy because she has a biblical understanding of joy. As I put my plans together, I will remind her of the lesson she presented on "The Joy of the Lord is Our Strength," from Beth Moore's *Living Beyond Yourself.* I would like for her to recap her vision of joy and share one of her memorable moments of joy that she and her brother shared with our family.

Obituary

You may say you want others to write your obituary and that's fine, but there are so many parts involved that it might not be complete. The *New York Times* interviews aging prominent people and does research in advance and has over 1,000 interviews on file for updating when a death occurs. Their obituaries are thorough and compelling. Consider viewing them and then writing an exit bio to serve as a summary of your life. Also, short and long obituaries can be read in local papers.

An obituary includes the announcement of death, a biographical sketch, information about the family, service times, special messages, and photos. This is a time to honor you and pay tribute to your life and your accomplishments. Celebrate the worthy parts of your life and your personality.

Before you determine if you want to write your obituary or have someone else write it, check with the newspaper and/or funeral home. Both provide forms for basic information and may write it for you. Starting with these steps may help you begin to write or gather information, or make decisions to include in your Life's End Journal.

Write your biographical information with locations of birth, marriage, and death, as well as predeceased and surviving loved ones' names, schools attended, military service, memorable places of employment and positions held, hobbies or special interests, and membership in civic, corporate, or fraternal organizations, or places of worship. Also, list the charities to which you would like donations to be sent. Add addresses and websites that may be useful.

Epitaph

You may have some personal descriptions of yourself that you have not spoken. Now is the time to write down a few words to honor yourself that will live forever on your marker. Write what you would want your family to see or just a stranger passing by.

Before you determine if you want to write your epitaph, consider that epitaphs are short and concise with the name and dates of birth and death. Mostly, they are written in the voice of the deceased.

Some Examples

"Free at Last. Free at Last. Thank God Almighty, I'm Free at last"—Rev. Dr. Martin Luther King, Jr.

"I will not be right back after the message."—Merv Griffin

"She did it her way."—Bette Davis

"Damn it's dark down here."—Fran Thatcher

Assignment

- In fifteen words or less, write two or three examples of words you want on your tombstone.

Chapter 10—Expectations from Journaling

"Do not conform any longer to the pattern of
this world, but be transformed by the renewing of your
mind. Then you will be able to test and approve
what God's will is—his good, pleasing and perfect will."

ROMANS 12:2

Prayer: Heavenly Father, I am trying to change my life to meet your standards. Help me to speak and write your word in manners that transform minds to understand your ways. Thank you for your good, pleasing, and perfect will. Amen.

TAKING HOLD OF YOUR life by journaling sets up the expectation that something specific is going to happen because you have designed the necessary courses of action. You are looking forward to realizing the dream that results from your plan.

We are waiting for everything to fall into place as we write forward in our journal about the action steps we are taking to get to the mountaintop. We believe God has a plan for us, as it is written in Jeremiah 29:11: "'For I know the plans I have for you,' declares the Lord, 'plans to prosper you and not to harm you, plans to give you hope and a future.'"

Christians have extraordinary expectations from God for their work in his service, as in his promises. First Corinthians 15:58 says, "stand firm. Let nothing move you. Always give yourselves fully to the work of the Lord, because you know that your labor in the Lord is not in vain." And Galatians 6:9 adds, "at the proper time we will reap a harvest if we do not give up."

As I have said, in my Write Forward Journal, there are three sections that I must write to address my work of the Lord: Spiritual Desires (remaining in Christ), Outreach (listing people to whom I witness in any way), and Goodness (my daily acts of goodness that helped someone). I shall write about how I seek him, how I represent him, and how I share the compassion he gives me for others.

If I put him first, there will be journal entries that are full of joyful expression about my book writing, traveling, meetings, finances, wellness, family, and friends. These writings will reflect God's blessings upon me, based on my desire to obey his word. This does not mean there will be no discomfort and sorrow, but if we persevere, we will see his wonders at work.

So, how do we know God's plan for our lives? Of utmost importance is the fact that we must have a relationship with him to the point that he can communicate with us and we can hear him. We must seek to know him and keep knocking at the door, asking for more and more of a relationship with him through prayer, reading his word, and trusting him. "Trust in the LORD with all your heart and lean not on your own understanding; in all your ways acknowledge him, and he will make your paths straight" (Prov 3:5–6).

We have all received gifts that are at work in our lives. Look at your being. What are you up to? What are you good at? That's what you're called to do.

In chapter 8, we addressed the past, present, and future, then decided what we wanted to do after we took hold of our lives. As we write in our Write Forward Journal, we must write meditations on our present lives and listen for him to speak to our hearts. And he will do so when we least expect it or daily at the same time. He speaks to me as I awake each morning, so then

I write his message or execute the task. Marvels like these bring clarity to his will for my life.

I pray that my dreams are aligned with his plan for me. In my Write Forward Journal, I am going to add a section called Tracking. I will list my dream steps as they come true and note how they were altered or how they are moved forward.

I look for signs of God working in my life that move my dream forward. Over the past two years, I've spoken to church groups and had opportunities to sell my books. Now in my Write Forward Journal, I am developing goals, taking specific steps, and moving forward toward my dream. I am trying to pay attention to the doors he opens and the doors he closes. Plus, I am learning to say no to activities that are outside my plans.

Ultimately, I want to be a woman who is so successful that the Holy Spirit is pleased to dwell in me. I want to go beyond wealth, fame, and power; I want to be successful in the sight of God, doing his will to accomplish whatever he wants me to do.

How will you know it is God's plan? It may feel like your dreams are not aligned with his. If you believe, ask. "If any of you lacks wisdom, you should ask God, who gives generously to all without finding fault, and it will be given to you. But when you ask, you must believe and not doubt, because the one who doubts is like a wave of the sea, blown and tossed by the wind" (Jas 1:5–6).

How will you know that God is answering? I believe he responds with "yes," "no," "not now," "I have a different plan," or "this blessing is not for you—it's for someone else." But you can listen by continuing your Write Forward Journal, watching for signs of his word and the Holy Spirit, and waiting for his response. "Wait for the LORD; be strong and take heart and wait for the LORD" (Ps 27:14).

I asked several people to respond to the question: "If I could take hold of my life, what would I do to make the rest of my years outstanding?" They answered:

Spend time with my grandchildren, teaching them family history and explaining to them why I made significant decisions in my life. *To accomplish this, I must move to a city closer to my grandchildren.*

Move to a condo where my husband and I can have separate bedrooms and bathrooms. *To accomplish this, we must sell our house and move to another neighborhood.*

Spend more time helping the less fortunate. Read to children. Hold the hand of a senior and let them know they are not alone. *To accomplish this, I would have to quit my job to have the flexibility to move about during the daytime.*

Spend more time with family. *To accomplish this, I would have to reorient my life's work.*

Pray more, love more, see others through the eyes of God, and watch my words by using them less to express myself. *To accomplish this, I would have to pray continually.*

Spend more time supporting young people and helping them and others understand that while having a bias is innate, it doesn't have to be a barrier to access, inclusion, and consideration. *To accomplish this, I would have to take time from my family to participate in specific academic courses and activities.*

Live debt-free. *To accomplish this, I would have to discipline myself to pay off all my bills and to create no new debt.*

Work to help others who are less fortunate by providing tangible resources for whatever their needs are. *To accomplish this, I would have to realign my finances and limit my spending on my family.*

Stand up for justice and practice compassion. *To accomplish this, I would have to transform my life to be in a position to demonstrate the need to promote positive actions.*

These replies clearly show that it would take time to accomplish their desires. As a result of the transformation, some aspects would be life-changing. They might require moving to another city, changing jobs, retiring, or an infusion of money. All would require them to pray continually to be able to carry on their magnanimous endeavors, because, "Whatever you do, work at it with all your heart, as working for the Lord, not for human masters" (Col 3:23).

Join me in this boundless journey. We have six journals or one journal with six sections:

1. Daily Journal
2. Therapeutic Journal
3. Spiritual Journal
4. Memoir Journal
5. Life's End Journal
6. Miscellaneous Journal

If we use our journals skillfully, we can sit back and write our way toward our destinations. We will pray continually. We will love plentifully. We will meditate in writing. We will cultivate a daily journaling regimen.

As a result, perhaps you may be the only real Christian that one person saw today and they noticed something that you did for someone else that made them think, "that person must be a Christian." When others see us as loving and compassionate people who stand above mediocrity in our actions, they may be drawn to the God we serve. In God's awesome wisdom, he chose to use you and me to help him spread the good word. While we are cooperating with God's plan, he will allow us to live out our ambitions in our day-to-day lives and become enormously complete, joyful, and purposeful.

> "His divine power has given us everything we need for a godly life through our knowledge of him who called us by his own glory and goodness" (2 Pet 1:3).

Epilogue

Psalm 23

"The Lord is my shepherd, I lack nothing.
He makes me lie down in green pastures,
he leads me beside quiet waters, he refreshes my soul.
He guides me along the right paths for his name's sake.
Even though I walk through the darkest valley,
I will fear no evil, for you are with me;
your rod and your staff, they comfort me.
You prepare a table before me
in the presence of my enemies.
You anoint my head with oil; my cup overflows.
Surely your goodness and love will follow me
all the days of my life,
and I will dwell in the house of the Lord forever."

The twenty-third Psalm summarizes what God will do if you believe. If you trust him, he will lead you. If you follow him, he will take you to a place of divine joy. If you commune with him, he will bless you abundantly as you stay with him for the rest of your life and into his kingdom.

You've read all 24,000 words of this book, completed the ten assignments, and now you're ready to *Journal It*. But, no matter how much you want to take hold of your life by journaling, it's hard to get started. Writing takes practice and consistency, as with anything new you want to pursue. Stick-to-it-iveness. It's hard to journal, especially if you don't have a habit of writing something with any frequency. But, you'll be surprised what goes from your mind, to your hand, through the pen and ink, and onto the paper.

Okay, so if you're not sure where to start, try journaling the first line. For example: "I want to get hold of my life and take it to a new level where I am at peace with my family and friends around me. When I am with them, I want to be intentionally present and totally engaged in the conversation, the sounds, the movements, and the feelings."

So, how do I get there?

This book gives you a clear five-step route with many choices—it is a guide to those who are journaling and are willing to write, read, rewrite, review, go live it, and "pray continually" (1 Thess 5:17).

But you must begin to write or speak into your journal about where you want to go. Again, you must begin, however small and halting the steps. Begin.

1. Select the pen, paper, and place, as well as where and when you will write or speak your journal. Where are you most comfortable writing and daydreaming?

2. Determine the purpose for your journaling. Do you want to write a memoir or map out the next five years of your life to achieve that special dream?

3. Outline the kind of journaling you want to implement. Your purpose may help you determine how to proceed. Do you need to view your old photo albums or cut out magazine articles that depict the future you?

4. Take control of your life through journaling by writing a short story about you from the past, you in the now and you in the future. What are the issues that concern you and impact your life?

5. Give yourself a timeframe within which to write in order to reach a point to reflect on how the journal is going. Should

you write more, rewrite, or start doing the things that are listed in the future?

Wrap it up with a perfect eulogy of good words about you and the epitaph for your headstone. "Give thanks in all circumstances; for this is God's will for you in Christ Jesus" (1 Thess 5:18).

Do something! Go for it!

My dream is to talk to people and convince them that, through journaling, they can change their lives. "You need to persevere so that when you have done the will of God, you will receive what he has promised" (Heb 10:36).

My personal plan is to write for five days about myself and how I feel and what I want for myself. For example, each day I will write and start with, "This is how I feel today. I feel blue and I want to explain why I feel blue."

Feeling blue aggravates my engagement. So, I must write until I can explain the blues away or clarify the blues. In addition to writing, I must be doing. To wash the blues away, I'm going to get dressed up and go see a beautiful movie that depicts all the things that make me smile, or maybe I'll sit home and watch my favorite movie on television.

Now, I am feeling good about myself, life, and people in general. I will volunteer to conduct classes on journaling and how it can impact your life. With my dream ready to begin, I must get back to writing as this is going well. I must write about what I've accomplished and plan for the class. We'll use my book as the text.

My journal now is becoming a complete course outline with real examples and opportunities for live input from the audience. Wow, by spring, in three months, I will have gotten hold of my life and done something I wanted to do. It all started with writing in my journal and remembering God's promise of faithfulness and his words of encouragement for the rest of my life. "These words are trustworthy and true. The Lord, the God who inspires the prophets, sent his angel to show his servants the things that must soon take place" (Rev 22:6).

This is not just a promise of rewards, but an incentive to live a godly life and share his word, known as the gospel. It is our inspiration and contains much advice for improvement.

Taking hold of your life through journaling represents an opportunity to create or prepare for something new. What we compose helps us get a handle on and understand our spiritual equilibrium. This life is preparing us for time everlasting as we live it with a view toward God's kingdom. As Revelation 22:12–13 says: "Look, I am coming soon! My reward is with me, and I will give to each person according to what they have done. I am the Alpha and the Omega, the First and the Last, the Beginning and the End." And yet we awaken each new day to "The bright and morning star" (Rev 22:16).

Benediction

Let us write in our journals, using awesome words that show how we experience his power in our lives. And while we are praying, we are anticipating that no matter what, HE will return again: "'Yes, I am coming soon.' Amen. Come, Lord Jesus" (Rev 22:20).

END

www.ingramcontent.com/pod-product-compliance
Lightning Source LLC
Chambersburg PA
CBHW071104090426
42737CB00013B/2464